TAX PLACEMENT

Tax Placement

Lawrance George Lux

iUniverse, Inc.
New York Lincoln Shanghai

Tax Placement

iUniverse, Inc.

For information address:
iUniverse, Inc.
2021 Pine Lake Road, Suite 100
Lincoln, NE 68512
www.iuniverse.com

ISBN: 0-595-27363-7 (pbk)
ISBN: 0-595-65671-4 (cloth)

Printed in the United States of America

Contents

Credits		*vii*
Preface		*ix*
CHAPTER 1:	INTRODUCTION	1
CHAPTER 2:	THE SUPPLY-SIDE ARGUMENT	9
CHAPTER 3:	THE DEBATE.	16
CHAPTER 4:	ELEMENTS OF CONSUMPTION	25
CHAPTER 5:	TAXES AND WHAT THEY DO.	37
CHAPTER 6:	TYPES OF TAXES	46
CHAPTER 7:	GENERAL FORMS OF TAXATION	54
CHAPTER 8:	IMPACT OF TAXES	63
CHAPTER 9:	THE WISH LIST	74
CHAPTER 10:	A GENERAL TAX SYSTEM	84
CHAPTER 11:	METHODOLOGY	91
Conclusion		99

Credits

The Author engages in online Internet discussions, as do almost all Readers. He has found valuable assistance in formulating his economic views from extended economic discussions at a Roundtable forum. These discussions allowed him to precisely formulate his thoughts, and understand the basic contradictory views to his own. Robert Liu provided intense discussion, presenting a masterful exposition of the Supply-Side Economic argument. Joseph Michael Kearney presented excellent Monetarist criticisms to the above discussions, in an unrelenting analytical format; based upon deep research. David Arthur Walters brought a depth of research to these discussions, with presentation of a Liberal view of Economics and Politics; which would be a credit to the most learned of Intellectuals. The end-result of the intermix of ideas exceeded any College Graduate Class discussion to which the Author has ever been a Participant.

The Author will here state all ideas presented in this Work are his own responsibility, of which the Above-mentioned should share in no slight for their utterance. The Individuals cited may even take offense from mention in this Work, and if so: I would most heartily apologize. I feel it is necessary, though, to mention their contribution in setting my own thoughts. I would also like to mention Matt Miller, who provides the Forum in which the above discussions could take place. Honorable mention must also be extended to Hanley Harding, Peter Benson, the adorable Claywoman—both in Intellect and Beauty, and other Entrants to discussions; who provided great speculations, moderation of bickering, and a sound approach to life for All on the discussion forum.

Lawrance George Lux
March 8, 2003

Preface

A wide variety of Economic theorists exist today; all generally divided along lines of how much Government should regulate the Economy. Further disruption enters the discussion, because all Economists have beliefs the Ideal should be modified to benefit certain segments of the Economy. A Case in Point could be the new Homeland Security bill, presently awaiting Presidential signature as the Author writes. Homeland Security enactment exhibits Supply-Side Economics willingness to utilize Government action to support their agenda, despite all philosophy.

The majority coalition supporting the Bill through the halls of Congress, consisted of Republican Supply-Side supporters. They tacked on several provisions to help Business: notably allowing Corporations moving off-shore to escape American taxes, to be allowed to bid on Government contracts. There was actually no limitation to these Corporations in the Bid process aforesaid; simply Government insistence these Corporations pay taxes on earned Profits from such Government contracts. The provision allows escape from such taxation. This provision was fully in accord with Supply-Side sentiment, which holds Government taxation of Business profits to be injurious to economic performance.

The other major provision placed in the Bill, though, was directly counter to the basic Supply-Side argument, which states Government should not regulate economic activity. This Provision forestalled Consumers from suing Drug companies for damages from supplied Vaccines. This is direct impediment of pre-accepted economic participant initiative; and direct evasion by Drug companies of responsibility for the quality of their product. They would use Government law to fore-stall redress, simply because it would affect business interests on the behalf of Consumers. This was hypocritical adoption of Government interference to protect business profits, in absolute denial of ideology.

Keynesianism can be equally hypocritical in political expression, refusing limitation on judgements against business in Civil Court actions; though it is recognized as unjust taxation, and detrimental to economic performance. They support usurious taxation of alcohol and tobacco, though realizing this is injurious to both Consumer and Business; with no proof existent that the medical costs of such usage equals the high assessments. They actually sponsor legislation allowing all medical costs to be magnified by around 400%, because it magnifies Government expenditure on Welfare programs. They are joined in this by their Economic opponents, because it is extremely profitable for the medical industry. The result is the same Pill sells for $.30 in foreign countries, while selling for $8 here; a wheelchair costing $1800 here, can be purchased elsewhere for $300. This is true when all Products are produced in the United States. Drugs companies are currently attempting to curtail free trade, because of American purchase of drugs from foreign distributors; an impediment to Drug companies' usurious Profits, with minuscule objection from Anyone.

Most current Economic argument asserts less Government interference in economic activity remains best for economic performance. Monetarists contend certain instruments of production, mainly financial resources, should be used to moderate economic performance; allowing overt Government interference to lapse. Supply-Siders insist Government interference should consist solely of activity to benefit and advance Business interests, believing Business profitability to be the well-spring of economic performance. Tax Policy Economists, of which the Author is one, believe Government interference can be damaging to economic performance by it's nature of bureaucratic regulation and ineffective distribution; thinking the imposition of taxes being the only correct realm for Government action in the Economy. Keynesianism still remains committed to massive Government control.

Monetarists equal control of the Banks, plus unrestrained Business interest. Supply-Siders desire unrestrained Business interest, with action taken to forestall Business liabilities and taxation. Keynesianism want massive Government regulation of business. Tax Policy Economists want judicious taxation to control the Economy, without ineffective Government regulation and regulatory costs. The above equates to the basic Economic theories currently operative, with Government action deriving from implementation of these theories, by venue of legislation. The interaction of all theories with their support, assures little occurs in the political arena to establish consistent rates of growth for the Economy.

A sad factor often arises from the process of Politics: The interaction of various economic theories to produce law, often adopts the worst of every theory; while canceling the beneficial aspects of any theory. The joining of Monetarist, Supply-Sider, and Keynesian has brought about the medical industry debacle in this Country, as noted above. Supply-Side conquest of the Keynesian Environmental Protection Agency has brought about the first lowering of Emission standards in the Agency's history, with no thought Power companies will use said Savings to reduce actual Emission levels; they possessing no incentive to do so. Monetarists have lowered Interest rates to practically nothing, yet the National Debt is rising; while actual Consumption and resultant Investment in hard Capital is dropping. Tax Policy Economists, specifically this Author, assert the policy is generating a new Stagflation.

This Book will attempt to prove the above argument. The Author will here give a short synopsis for those who would not read further. Levels of Consumption are dropping because of current economic uncertainty; because of rising Unemployment due to Business downsizing, deficit Government spending on all three levels of Government, and rising Consumer prices—Inflation. Business is not capitalizing production facilities, due to the falling Consumption. Monetarist theory will work to promote Consumption only if it is not canceled by an Inflationary rate over 1.3%. This condition is only worsened by Credit Card companies and financial institutions refusal to lower Consumer Credit rates. The lowered Prime rates only allow Business to refinance at lower rates than the debt was originally capitalized, and allow the financial institutions to refuse to lower Consumer Credit rates by marginal Profit gains to themselves. Monetarist theory has already lost all ability to affect the Economy. The Author uses a rule of thumb concerning the use of Monetarist theory; considering Credit extension pressure for an Inflation rate of 1.3%. He suggests the Prime interest rate must be at least 3.9%, or three times the potential Inflation rate; in order for Consumption to be maintained due to erosion of profitability of financial instruments.

The Bush Tax Cut stands as the joy of Supply-Side Economists. Business taxes were reduced to practically nothing, with many Corporations given Rebates for taxes they did not even pay initially. The National Debt began to balloon, and would have done so; even without the Sept. 11th Attacks with the War on Terrorism. The Business tax reductions have not led to capital investment, due to reduced Consumer Demand; they have simply allowed Business and Corporation to refinance at lower Interest rates, and maintain current Price schedules because of maintained Profits. The Bush Tax Cut actually impedes normal economic performance, because it supplies inelasticity to Price schedules. It also creates National Debt because of unfunded Government operations, draining assets from a financial market; already losing it's aggregation facility due to lowered Interest rates. The Tax Cut does not promote the Economy, as it curtails Consumption; with hard capital construction reduced from loss of that Consumption. Economic conditions actually call for Tax increases to promote Economic activity.

1

Introduction

Tax incidence or placement stands as a difficult subject for any Author; most finding Examples outweighing discussion, or dialogue so obtuse the Reader is lost. The Subject, though, must be understood by the general population; it vitally affects their interaction within the Economy. Almost All understand taxation, while necessary to underwrite Government expenditure, has adverse effects upon the productivity of the Economy. Few realize Tax incidence can do five times the damage, as does the simple withdrawal of assets from the Production process. Tax placement has been known to bring down even the most robust Economy, through constriction of key elements of the Production process.

Most discussion of Tax policy with incidence revolves around distribution of wealth concepts. Liberal Economists advocate use of Tax to redistribute wealth in the Economy, basically by extraneous tax levels on the wealthier Income-earners, to provide funding for welfare transfers to the Poor. The Rationale for such transfers insist lower Incomes derive from lack of economic opportunity for these socially-disadvantaged classes. Liberals assert lower Incomes could attain the same Income levels as wealthier Incomes, if they had the same advantages of decent housing, education, dietary standards, and job availability. The Author joins Conservatives, who claim the argument is faulty. There are distinct differences in labor performance completely unbiased by childhood experience; some of the most successful of the WWII Generation came from seriously disadvantaged households. Most of the disadvantaged of succeeding Generations have had the minimum advantages of the best of the aforementioned Generation.

The basic Conservative assessment states wealthier Incomes do not, and should not, have any responsibility for the economic position of poorer elements in Society. They assert the process of earning an improved economic position develops the Individual, nothing but the hard process of economic employment allows for the skill development inducing higher Income levels. There is inherent truth in this assertion, though the argument ignores the actuality 95% of wealthier classes lack the skill development necessary to have earned the wealth they inherited from their forebears; a excellent argument for high inheritance tax levels, to induce development of skill levels. It still stands as valid an economic participant must develop such skills to attain an improved position, if they were not lucky in choice of competent forebears. Welfare transfers show few advantages gained for Recipients in the economic realm, simple provision of a minimum standard of living alone. This provision often blocks economic incentive, through threat of loss of economic underwriting upon working.

Actual Economic record indicates such Welfare transfers actually create dependency among Recipients, making them less capable of handling the rigors of the economic sphere. The heavy emphasis on Education already expresses a massive real salary reduction for College graduates, with massive addition to Graduate-level education; simply to reach real salary remuneration equivalent to past Generations of college graduates. Most Economists would insist this effect comes from the greater necessary technological expertise of Today's economy; but the Author would claim it is the loss of skill levels of College graduates, MBAs currently exhibiting only a quarter of the skills of prior Generation Masters of Business Administration graduates. It expresses a loss of educational standards for provision of inclusion to the educational process (a regrettable Keynesian proposition).

The Social Security Administration probably highlights the worst aspects of Welfare transfers. The average Social Security beneficiary probably draws twice the monthly income which he had, after taxation during his work years; due to Cost of Living increases. The idea such beneficiaries paid for their retirement remains a fallacy. They could not have paid for their benefits, even under the benefit program existent when they were paying into the Fund. The idea this tendency will reverse with the higher earnings of the Present workers after their retirement—allowing benefits to be less of a percentage total of household income, also joins the ranks as doubtful. Their contributions cannot even fund the current benefit payments of the current recipients, fewer in number. Economists protest the above argument, but the Author uses total income averaging across the entire work history of the beneficiaries. The argument will remain equally valid into the future with expanded numbers across the board; predicated by Cost of Living increases.

Medicare stands as the greatest expression of the doubtful quality of Welfare transfer payments. Medical insurance premiums prior to the inception of the Medicare program in the 1960s were approximately equivalent per year, to the monthly premiums demanded for Medicare Supplement insurance today. Full medical insurance underwriting, not just Supplemental to Medicare, requires six to seven times such payment per month. Actual cost of health care has increased at about four times the Inflation rate, coincident with Insurance processing cost increases of almost two thousand percent; this during the Period of Computer development, where administrative costs were supposed to decline. The Cause of such huge increase comes from an entire industry development, for the sole purpose of absorbing such welfare transfers; with little concern for real improvement of health care. The Author, and many medical specialists, insist the quality of health care has declined; with the introduction of the Profit motive into Health care.

The first point of this Work has been made! The Author doubts the viability of the use of Taxation as a wealth redistribution program. Welfare transfers will always develop economic structures designed to absorb such financial payments, a provision of service not dedicated to Welfare recipients; but only to obtaining economic positioning for themselves. Assets are acquired by these economic structures and employees, leaving little improvement of economic opportunity for the designated Welfare recipients. The Poor and Disadvantaged fail to gain, because they still lack participation in the economic process. The best case in point are the Social Security recipients, who are unlikely to be better off than their Grandparents at like age; though they are paid an immense amount for supported services.

Taxes should not be accessed or placed for the purpose of redistribution of wealth. Such programs simply incite the growth of economic structures which are undesirable, generate a high inflationary pressure, and create an employed class to service such transfers; which is nothing but parasitism based upon Government expenditure. Reordering economic performance in order to eliminate excess charges for economic activities becomes difficult, due to the employment levels of this parasitic industry; such industries always with effective political lobbies. Such parasitic industry charges are almost certain to have caused Sixty percent of Inflation, since the inception of Medicare in the 1960s.

The basic role of Taxes must be kept in sight at all times: Taxes are raised to fund Government expenditures. Politics determine what those expenditures should consist of, always increasing as Politicians promise more to the Citizenry. It is the duty of Economists to educate this self-same Citizenry as to the hazards of excessive Government expenditures. They can do this in two basic ways: by explanation of the horrors of poor Tax policy; and by expressing the fallacy of Government expenditure programs. Neither initiative shows much influence in raising public understanding, as they are continually opposed by a structured Political propaganda machine dedicated to misleading the Public. Politicians insist on expanding Public opinion as to the value of their efforts, though those efforts are most often more injurious than helpful.

Like analysis to the above discussion of Welfare transfer payments describe the fallacy of Government expenditure programs. Filtration of funds through a growing parasitic service industry, will always brings reduction of real advantage to every Welfare transfer system. The economic position financial needs are served, rather than the needs of Recipients; who find steadily reducing advantage from the welfare programs. Increases of funding to the welfare program only enriches the parasitic service industry and it's employees, without materially increasing the benefit to Recipients(only matching Inflation). The general populace must be made to comprehend, Government welfare programs serve only Politicians and parasitic service industries; failure to provide this enrichment, would lead to a dismantlement of the welfare program. This enrichment forestalls any material advantage accruing to the Recipient class, because of their lack of participation in the economic process.

This Work endures as an attempt to explain the role of Taxation in the Economy, explaining it's effective economic functioning to the Reader. Tax policy affects the whole of the Economy. Excessive taxation reduces Consumption rates, retards the aggregation of capital for Investment, and generates excessive Government expenditure. The latter is most noted by rapidly expanding program budgets, increased benefits for Government employees, and rapidly expanding Pork projects; petty programs specifically to generate support for Politicians in their bids for reelection. The astute Economist classifies all of the above as simply Cosmetic, as these processes do nothing to further the proscribed goals of Government programs; at increasing cost to the tax-paying Public. Too little taxation brings Deficits, unfunded Infrastructure costs, environmental hazards, and indifferent security for the Public.

Tax placement or incidence can be equally destructive. Erroneous placement of tax can discriminate against specific class segments among economic participants, causing their loss of economic gain from such participation. Poor Tax placement can eliminate the ability to Save for many economic participants, causing them to lose a capital formation possibility. Many lose ability to alter economic performance, because excessive Tax placement precludes entrance into gainful opportunities. This, though, is basically all on an Individual level; not particularly of great economic consequence, although of immense damage to the suffering.

Bad tax incidence contributes to the loss of economic viability for entire classes of the economy, this due mainly to wrongful types of taxation. Wealthier classes use specific types of taxation, to limit participation of lower classes in the economic decision-making process. Such taxes can be used to insure little capital accumulation for poorer classes. They can be used to assure poorer Incomes must pay for Government expenditure, allowing higher Incomes to escape paying their fair share. They can be used to get poorer classes to underwrite Costs, which higher Incomes would have to bear, if the Poor did not pay through taxation; case in point, residential Property-tax payers underwrite eighty percent of the infrastructure access costs of business in this Country. This deliberate mal-adjustment of tax incidence endures heavy resistence to change, as higher Incomes enjoy greater influence with political authorities.

The above paragraph implies the Author feels the wealthier classes are totally responsible for misplacement of Taxes. This is patently untrue! The greatest malefactor in the malignancy of tax incidence consists of inconsistent attention. Tax systems evolved over a great length of time, with little effective study of their various impacts. People consider a Tax like unto the weather, something to avoid if possible; but unalterable. It is hard disparaging a thing which has been in operation for decades or centuries. It stands as even harder to speculate on adverse consequences, when people have lived with those consequences as a part of their entire lives. The Economist faces a reaction which dismisses disparagement as groundless complaint.

The task becomes overwhelmingly great, as the Economist must provide evidence first that alternatives are available; stipulate specific changes which could be made, then go on to quantify the potential advantages to be gained by change. The Reader might believe the effort is done at this point, but it only begins at this level of involvement. Tax systems are a part of the fabric of every Economy. Every alteration, no matter how minor it be, produces Winners and Losers by such change; all of whom will have advocates at Court in the political process. The Economist must prove there would be far more Winners than Losers, and then hope the Winners possess more political clout than do the Losers. The Reader should understand Tax policy alteration comes slow in the political environment, where political leadership responds actively to political protest. It does not help that political leadership is almost always derived from the wealthier classes, when such Tax change could adversely affect wealthier elements of the Economy.

The cartography of Tax systems breeds great obstruction to any efforts for change. The Charters for Tax systems reside in often multiple extensions of original law, with multiplex alterations of minute order; all in order to specifically please some Power broker or Interest. Basic Tax alteration affect all such extensions, nullifying all these entrenched subsidies. The Reformer finds immediate massive opposition. The specific text of the original law and it's extensions insure need for legalistic skill, or competent legal counsel, able to provide language in proper legal phraseology; in order to cancel previous legislation without legal contest. It remains certain this legal contest will be fully-funded, and capable of durative combat.

Such Conflict picks up immediate support from the technicians of the old Tax system, those who made a living by implementing and collecting the previous tax. They are often enfranchised by Civil Service regulation, so they cannot be fired or unwillingly transferred. The maintained employment incites an economic cost, which nullifies a great share of the economic gain generated by the Tax alteration. They underwrite their opposition with extensive political clout, having worked closely with the political leadership in their employment.

The Economist finally must face the opposition of the greatest majority of the Citizenry, who have a facility for immediate notice of tax increases; but rarely acknowledge tax reductions. This means Citizens, who do not understand the new tax alterations, will oppose the increase of taxes in those areas where taxes are increased; without understanding or admission their tax burden has been reduced elsewhere. The burden of informing the Citizenry, therefore, falls to the Reformer; an expense hard to bear without active support.

Tax policy enters a destructive phase at this point, where only reductions of tax on Business interests and the Wealthy possess the innate support for passage. Such a combination of forces often oppose tax alteration, even conscious of the overall benefit to the Economy; simply because it adversely affects their own position. Economist must often raise an entire Generation of children with education as to the benefits of tax change, before such changes will be realized.

2

The Supply-Side Argument

The basic Supply-Side argument developed in the 1960s-70s, with much Conservative backlash criticism for Keynesian economics of Big Government and huge expenditures. A major feature of their opposition was the ballooning National Debt, which they attributed to Welfare transfer programs initiated since the FDR administration. They derided the Keynesian concept of Government spending fueling the Economy, insisting the process of cutting taxes allowed Business and Consumer to readjust their economic participation for peak economic performance. The concept of deficit spending was not dismissed as economic fuel, simply transferred from Government expenditure to unpaid taxes. Effective Government economic participation claimed to come in the form of reducing Business risks and costs, and issuing lucrative Contracts for military defense and Infrastructure.

The underlying premise of Supply-Side argument came in the form: Anything which reduced the total costs of Production, was the greatest incentive to economic performance. This allowed for rapid capital formation, with the claim of promoting development. Supply-Side Economists oppose any Business taxation, stating it drains the economic incentive for development. They insist the complete burden for Government expense should be borne by the Consumer, through personal income tax or excise tax. They imply this removal of Business tax would be the best economic fuel.

The Supply-Side Economists came to power with the Reagan administration. They immediately began to implement their basic philosophy. The incomes of Business people began to rapidly expand, while the incomes of Wage-earning Consumers started to decline. The National Debt embarked on an period of immense increase. The Economy tanked. Consumption engendered was minuscule in growth rates. Everyone was living worse, except for the Business community; and Government welfare commitments soared. Supply-Siders claimed success, because of the increase of Business profits; dismissing reduced Consumption as due to Labor re-allocations without pay, and increased Government spending to be removed by elimination of welfare programs.

The first anomaly expressed itself. Business was not utilizing their new-found wealth for capital formation. Consumption, while mostly not actually declining, was not growing; at least not at rates which justified massive capital construction in the limited market. The Age of Corporate Takeovers was born, where accumulated funds were used to purchase Consumer markets in other industries. The Sale price of Corporations skyrocketed, as competition to invest massive amounts of financial capital impelled higher purchase pricing. Corporations absorbed smaller Corporations, at great cost to the Purchaser; and great capital gains for selling Management and Stockholders. Purchasing Corporations found they had to increase Product prices, to show a Profit on the purchased Corporations. Consumption of these products slowed even more, due to the shrinking income of the Consumers and higher prices.

All Business personnel found themselves with a wealth of financial assets, without capitalization outlets; whether they were Corporations with untaxed wealth, or selling Management and Stockholders. The deposits in Banks and S&Ls flowered at geometric rates. These financial institutions faced a huge dilemma; they could lower their lending rates drastically, or loosen the conditions for making loans with less collateral and proven profitability. The Business community, with increasing deposits in financial institutions, pressured the Federal Reserve to maintain Interest rates.

Financial institutions instigated new rules for extending Credit. The Age of Mall Building began; with vast Retail outlets and Office Rentals being constructed. Reality began to set in, as Malls were empty of Shoppers, and small Retailers could not afford the huge Rents for location in the Malls; the Rent rates demanded to avoid default on the construction loans. The Office Plazas had no Renters, who did not want to leave their spacious, lower-priced, convenient access to their Customers. The Age of Default commenced, leading to the S&L debacle; only narrowly avoiding a total Bank meltdown. The first great Supply-Side experiment failed.

The first error in Supply-Side Economics showed clearly; Government efforts to spur economic performance by Business tax cuts, cannot operate without actual physical identification of Consumer Demand. There has to exist a Consumer for present Products, before Business can be expected to invest expensively in new capital formation for expanded Production. The Consuming dollars must be there, held by willing Consumers. Both conditions must be present, else economic maladjustment occurs. Neither were present during the Supply-Side control of the 1980s.

The Tax Cuts of the Reagan administration cut the taxes of the least likely to Consume, as they were already supplied fully under their existing budgeted Consumption schedules. Those who would have increased their Consumption schedules with substantial tax cuts, did not receive effective tax cuts which would have increased Consumption. The Consuming dollars were there, but held by Individuals unwilling to increase Consumption. Those desirous of increasing their Consumption schedules could only do so with high-interest Credit. Business did not invest in production-increasing investment, because of high difficulty in selling current levels of Product.

The Reagan administration thought to expand the Economy under economic conditions, which did not propel economic expansion. Consumer Demand could not expand to absorb new Product, all because the potential Consumer was impeded by low Wage and high-interest Consumer Credit. Business, faced with a lack of expansion in Sales, thought to expand the Marketing infrastructure; with the hope of expanding Sales with an updated Marketing network. This failed because of the lack of Consuming dollars held by willing Consumers. The Marketing network, itself, retarded growth of Consumer Demand; as it magnified Costs at the Retail level, forcing up Product prices. The financial crisis only reflected the unrealistic economic projections utilized in the Government policy.

The election of George W. Bush allowed the Supply-Side argument to try once more. They re-introduced elimination of Business taxation, even to the point of giving Rebates for taxes never paid. The National Debt has again started to rise drastically, and all indications point to debt acceleration. Consumer Consumption levels are starting to slow and reverse, due to financial institutions' refusal to lower Consumer Credit interest charges; even though the Federal Reserve has reduced it's Prime rates to less than two percent. There has been no indication of capital investment expansion, rather; real evidence Business is downsizing with the Unemployment rate increasing, and retention of older equipment—slowing the Recapitalization rate. Business is re-financing it's Operating Capital and Mortgages through the lowered Fed rates; utilizing this added increase of funds to prop up and fix Product price schedules, further curtailing Consumption. Tax has again shifted the Consumer Dollar to the wrong hands; destroying the willingness of Consumers, and maintaining excessive Product price schedules.

Little real effort has been published studying the causes of the Reagan Recession; most Supply-Siders actually denying it's recessionary aspect. This contains regret, as the reinsertion of like economic policies will generate another Recession in the later Bush administration. The economic conditions for Stagflation have been rebuilt: Government deficit spending, loss of Consumption, aging of capital equipment, and rising Unemployment. Business is rebuilding a high financial liquidity, which they insist on moving to the financial markets. Tax revenues are dropping rapidly, as Consumers lose the marginal income of Overtime hours, increasing Consumer and Property taxes, and increasing Necessity Costs—like Utilities, Communications, and Education. This last means Consumers are losing their discretionary income, which is the heaviest component of Consumer finance.

Fundamental Supply-Side arguments states Government economic policy should be limited to the promotion of business interests, through elimination of Business taxes, and limitation of Business liabilities. It contends only Business interests possess the on-site knowledge to effectively regulate the Production process. It claims Government regulation can only interfere with the natural distribution process, as this regulation must always be pre-dated on obsolete information. Supply-Siders steadfastly refute any role for Government, Worker, or Consumer; outside of the role of Purchaser of product. They accept amendment of this statement to propel Government to grant them immunity from liability, for any irresponsibility of their part.

Supply-Side argument basically adopts Monetarist economic policy for the provision of Consumer Demand. Monetarists assert control of the financial instruments for provision of Consumer Credit, can produce the necessary Consumption levels to fuel the Economy. Both fields of thought ignore the primary role of Employment, in producing the necessary Consumption dollars. Financial institutions will not extend Credit, where there is no provision for repayment. Monetarists cannot get financial institutions to reduce Consumer Credit charges below a certain minimum, one determined by adequate return and expected levels of Inflation. They also cannot gain Credit extension for those who lack the ability to repay loans. Monetarists have attempted to raise the Credit/Wage ratio for decades, but cannot get the concurrence of financial institutions. Bankers insist on repayment to the point where they demand bankruptcy laws be modified, so debtors cannot avoid repayment of Consumption credit.

Supply-Side activity does not promote Consumer Demand, in and of itself. It asserts Production at the lowest possible cost must be the end-goal of the Economy. It lobbies Government for elimination of Business taxes, throwing the entire load for Government expenditures on Personal Incomes which underwrite all Consumer Consumption, as contretemps capital purchases for production. They do this though Business produces three-quarters of the Transportation infrastructure costs, one-third of the law enforcement costs, and 85% of the regulatory costs. Public costs of provision of labor forces are denied. The Supply-Side argument insists the Consumer should be grateful to pay the full cost of Government expenditures, while Business pay the lowest possible Wage; all to generate the highest possible Profits off of sale of Products, which are deliberately overpriced for aggregation of capital—unused for actual expansion of product provision, employment, or living standards.

Supply-Siders contend Business should not have responsibility for Product safety, training of labor reserves, or provision of welfare services; while they reserve the right to pay the minimum wage necessary to obtain labor. They desire Business immunity from Civil Tort, freedom from Corporate Income, Capital Gains, and Property taxes, elimination of Social Security and Unemployment Insurance contributions, and freedom from Excise tax on capital goods. They do favor limitation of Personal Income tax rates to levels less than their own personal incomes, with a raft of tax credits given for their normal conduct of operations.

The Supply-Side argument maintains Business resources must be left free to be manipulated, as the Market would dictate. They would see repeal of Insider Trading legislation, Contract limitations, and legislation demanding ethical rules of Conduct. They desire the disenfranchisement of the Environmental Protection Agency, and all antipollution regulation. Their contention states they can best regulate themselves, as they are involved in the industry; and can best determine the levels of protection necessary, though they are inevitably caught in malfeasance to increase Profits for their business entities. The record of Business dealing with ethical issues, especially the ones cited above, has been dismal in the economic history of the United States. What regulation which does exist, originated in corrupt malfeasance practiced by Business, at the time of inception.

A Case in point could be the latest Bush initiative to roll back the pollution standards for the Power plants. The decision immediately retards a necessary industry, the producers of anti-pollution controls; who will be impoverished and left without the capital return necessary for development. Approximately one hundred thousand workers will lose lucrative employment from this decision, without ability to obtain gainful employment in a like field. The Power plants in question are exceedingly old structure, which have taken their Recapitalization deductions throughout their operation; so Corporations owning such facilities have already acquired about four times the cost of replacement of the facilities in tax remissions. The Bush decision allows them to continue taking such tax remissions. The failure to introduce anti-pollution equipment will mean they will not be able to meet the new standards within four years, as current anti-pollution equipment wears out. Smog levels will increase by an estimated thirteen percent in surrounding areas, within a year. New plant facilities would replace current plants within five years, had the old standards remained in place, operating at eighty percent of the cost of current plants; and emitting forty percent of the particulate. The older plants will probably be in operation another twenty years, because of the Bush Decision.

3

The Debate.

Supply-Side argument proclaims economic performance will be maximized by the burden of tax being placed upon the Consumers, allowing Business to aggregate financial resources for capitalization purposes. They cite Monetarist claim financial liquidity for Consumption can be maintained by ease of Consumer Credit, and will remain consistent; as long as credit terms are sufficiently liberal. Both fields of Economic thought tend to ignore the actuality of necessary Consumption funding. Credit cannot be extended where there is no possibility of repayment. Each fondly imagine the Consumption process generates it's own income, but no one pays wages for the process of Consumption alone, the Services industries operating on minimum wages except in the Professions, unequal to production of discretionary income necessary for heavy Consumption buying. Credit repayment comes only from Wages or Savings. Social Security and other Welfare transfer payments hide the extreme lack of Consumption paid by Savings, it can be estimated less than fourteen percent of all Consumption could actually be funded by Savings; said Consumption could not be realized in the absence of substantial Income from Wage, Rent, Royalty, or Profit.

The importance of Labor Income shines dramatically. The Author speculates the Consumption pattern of the Grey Generation would decrease by over forty percent, with elimination of monthly Social Security benefits; this outlined by traditional Consumer reactions to substantial reductions of pooled Savings on a repeating basis. Re-implantation of daily payment of expenses out of the Savings of the Grey Generation would sharply curtail Consumption; Savings shrinking, un-replaceable financial assets permanently lost. Bombardment of medical expenses and premiums on an Age bracket highly susceptible to medical needs would bring an additional thirty percent loss in their Consumption pattern; with loss of Medicare payments. The Author is probably the only Economist, who asserts the Social Security program is a Consumption preservation program; containing few elements of welfare transfers to the Poor. Alteration reduction of the Consumption pattern of the Elderly of this magnitude could reduce total Consumption in this Country, by as much as One-Quarter.

One will find little Supply-Side or Monetarist argument against the Social Security programs, whether they realize the factors outlined by the Author or not. They do realize the combined political weight of all such Recipients; who do realize what loss of such Benefits would do to their lifestyle. The fallacy of current sentiment against Welfare transfer payments by Conservatives provides amusement, with the understanding such payments preserve Consumption patterns at present levels, of even the wealthier elements of society. Full-scale economic modeling has not been conducted in the area, but it can be estimated said wealthy Recipients would reduce their Consumption some $1.75-3.50, for each $1 of loss benefit; if said funds had to come from irreplaceable Savings. Loss of Medicare benefits, because of the extreme levels of fund retraction for medical expense, could raise the ratio up to $7 loss of Consumption for each dollar loss of medical payment. Millionaires would even probably cut their Consumption.

Republican Congressmen closed the current legislative Year with refusal to extend Unemployment benefits, insuring hundreds of thousands of Unemployed would lose a weekly income of some few hundred dollars per month. They did so feeling righteous in stopping such blatant welfare transfer of Wealth. Economic projection of effect would indicate almost $3.25 loss of Consumption, for every denial of a dollar. They proclaim the need for rugged Individualism, and the Unemployed need find alternate Income. This is in conformance with their Business mentality. The Downside may also affect their Business mentality; the numbers of Unemployed, with the loss of weekly income to pay for life expenses; could cause a loss of total Consumption of over 1.75 percent, over the period of one year. This loss of Consumption could lead to the unemployment of an additional Two percent of the national labor force.

The Republican Congress has since thought to restore Unemployment benefits, after the Christmas season of dismal Sales caused them to rethink the Process. The loss of Retail sales, though, was not the sole determinant for the restoration of benefits. Additional pressure was applied by industries of heavy Lobbyist weight, these being Utilities; they alarmed by the sharp rise in number of unpaid or delayed payment of monthly bills. There was a quick reevaluation of the utility of Unemployment benefits, as it started to impact industry.

Economists ofttimes lose sight of economic basics, while drifting around inside their economic theories. Recessive economic conditions can be stated as simple slowing of business activity, causing a loss of Profitability to Management and Labor. It must be stated clearly this slowing of Business activity begins with a reduction of participation of the Consumer in the Economy by reduced Consumer Demand and Consumption. A simple Overview of the Process can provide great light to the subject; also interjecting some economic proof of theoretical fallacies of current Economic thought.

Recessive economic conditions are caused by slowed business activity. This slowed activity is always foreshadowed by growth of Product inventories, the growth of these Inventories the simple result of lessened Consumer spending. Business reaction is to reduce productive hours, cut back on capital investment, lay off marginal labor, and resist Wage demands. This is only the first stage of their Reaction, and consists solely of efforts which have the affect of reducing Labor earnings. This loss of earnings by Labor is translated in reduced levels of Consumption on the part of Labor, as their Discretionary Income has been dissipated at a much higher rate than their Total Income; such discretionary funds coming from marginal income of full personal employment. Non-discretionary Income makes up almost no Consumption by Labor, as these funds go to pay for housing, heating, food, and utilities; which are absolutely necessary payments, and incapable of major deferment. Loss of eight hours of labor per Week can cause loss of 70% of Discretionary Income, with an almost equal loss of Consumer spending.

Increased Business Product inventories were initially caused by insufficient Consumption levels, which Business worsens by their first stage Reaction. They do this by withdrawal of Discretionary Income from Labor. Insufficient Consumption alters to dropping Consumption. Business thinks to counteract this effect, by introduction of Credit extension. They promise credit to distribution outlets, so these outlets will maintain their marketing personnel; though the productivity of marketing personnel drops. They pressure Credit agencies to lower Consumer interest rates, in hopes Consumers will increase their level of Debt. Labor is resistant to this expansion, if required repayment funds extend beyond relatively sustained, reliable Income sources. Labor is only fifteen percent as likely to incur increasing debt levels, outside mandatory lifestyle maintenance, during Recessive conditions; as they are under expectation of increasing Income levels. The ease of Consumer Credit does not work under Recessive conditions, unless the Credit extension was draconian previously. Business still does not find a market for it's Product.

The third and final stage of Business Reaction comes in reduction of Wholesale Product pricing, with decreasing profit per unit. Business delays in extending to this stage of reaction, because it directly affects their own business funding. Loss of Profitability incites loss of capital aggregation, lower Dividend payments to Stockholders, and loss of salaries to Management. The third stage remains the only reactive action conducive to increased levels of Consumption. It creates only long-term increments in Consumption, because of the previous action taken in the prior two stages. The Discretionary Income of Labor had already been reduced in a previous period, and Business almost never adopts the last stage of Reaction; until the Consumption pattern of Labor has already been reorganized. Business has already staged numerous marketing Sales of little import, because of previous refusal to reduce the Wholesale pricing of Product; leading to cynicism among Consumers (who boycott Retail outlets when they feel they do not have the economic viability to spend), and by prior draining of the profitability of the Retail industry. The consistent previous record of reduced Income, causes Credit agencies to reduce Consumer Credit extension to Labor; to levels below Any which could threaten repayment.

The reduction of Wholesale Product pricing was delayed beyond the Window, where such savings to Consumers could have jump-started renewed Consumption levels. Labor once again has to reconstitute their Discretionary Income levels, realistically done only by paying down their overall debt level; in the face of restrictive Business employment practices which will not provide marginal income levels. This 'paying down' of previous debt levels stands dependent upon maintenance of sufficient Income levels to reduce this debt, which cannot be done, if Business retains too restrictive a employment practice. A marked hazard of this Process comes in the form of reduced Housing sales, with coinciding loss of profitability for the Construction industry.

Economists, one and all, call for increased Government spending at this point, to spur the Economy. Almost All call for deficit spending, though the Author does not. Government spending is not the panacea which Most claim, for a number of reasons. Almost all Government expenditures are squandered on paying the life expenses of the Poor; a laudable endeavor, but providing only marginal production for the Economy. Pressure is always great to minimize Wage levels in Government programs, to employ the maximum number of workers. It is again provision of life maintenance costs; with little Discretionary

Income generated among all Participants. Business inventories are only minimally reduced. The accumulation of Government debt actually pressures reduction in Consumption, as will be proven in a following Chapter. The scope of Government expenditure actually maintains ease of employment for middle management personnel, as they switch to Government supervisory position; this process, though, drains effort to reorganize the Production function, as well as draining impetus for change by protecting the Incomes of the elites in the Production arena.

The first sign of Recessive conditions propels a 'knee-jerk' reaction of political and financial preferments for Business interests, which no one suggests should be withdrawn at the reinstatement of effective economic performance. The entirety of the Tax Burden today rests effectively on Personal Income, Consumption, and Residential Property ownership. Business is favored by Government, Utilities, and Resource Management. The inequity is of concern, but other aspects contain greater weight to the Economist. These need to be examined.

Government expenditure in the Economy is very great. It fluxes between about seventeen percent during Boom times, to about twenty-four percent under Recessive conditions. This differs remarkably from the eight to fourteen percent of the Economy, as was consistently present prior to the Second World War. There has been serious economic speculation this high level of expenditure is actually injurious to economic performance. The devotion of resources and skills to Government expenditure obviously reduces the level of Private Sector product; eliciting a greater Price schedule for such production, than normal Government expenditures would cause. The level of employment in provision of Government services obviously raises the Wage scales of all Employment, as only about half of this labor is directed to provision of funding for private Consumption. Government consumption of resources in their expenditures stands on the high end of the scale; demanding resource provision as first in line, vastly inflating the price of resource provision. The last causes the Government to pay excessive Wage scales, and directly forces up all Resource prices for all in need of such resources.

Much debate has been recorded on the value of Keynesian fuel of the Economy, for the purpose of increasing economic performance. The Author has never been an advocate of Keynesian theory, believing Government expenditure was always mis-allocated to advance economic performance; and could never be properly allocated, due to the context of massed political participation under which such allocations are made. The economic determinations of various theorists are of no moment, under the present discussion. The level of Government expenditure reduces the above argument in importance, as factors of magnitude intrude.

Whatever impact Keynesian fuel could have on economic performance has been nullified by the level of Government expenditure in the economy. The Government, by it's level of expenditure which averages twenty percent consistently in the current Age, has become the propellent of Inflation in both Resource prices and Wages. Economics remains a basic evaluation of balances: between Price and Quantity Supplied, between Consumption and Capital accumulation, and between Production and Sales. Enhanced Keynesian policies of Deficit spending, whether Supply-Side support of Business or Welfare transfers, will dis-balance the Economy in the direction of Recession; causing less Quantity Supplied with lower Capital investment, under artificially inflated Wages. The political opposition to remission of previous economic incentives introduced under Recessive conditions, preclude any capacity for Keynesian deficit spending by Government providing economic incentive in the future.

Business interests will be angered by the statement economic incentives to promote Business must be removed, before effective economic performance can be realized. Tax credits for Investment allow for over-consumption of Resource by Business, who does not have to bear the full brunt of resource-pricing. Delayed-payment Tax schedules allow Business and Investor to utilize reduced Cost, by utilization of Inflation. The Consumer is left to pay the Taxes, compete in a Resource market with artificially-empowered Competitors, and bear the full brunt of the Inflation caused by such activity and Government spending.

Technological advance operates to reduce Labor participation in the Economy; bringing huge advances in production with less Labor hours employed. These Labor hours are additionally higher-order educational skills; requiring enhanced training expense for employment. Actual Labor resources reduce in number, with greater intensity of Labor preparation. Current Business incentives actually counteract the current development, refusing to fund this advanced training or reward Employees for the training attainment through enhanced Wages. This economic loss compounds by placing the tax burden for Education on the Consumer.

Education has become intrinsically more expensive with longer duration of training, and increased educational aids. Business has sought through political means, to remove itself from funding of educational facilities; by Property tax shelter and increased Public funding of Education through taxation. They seek further tax shelter from contribution to general Public funds, so family households are left to bear the tax burden of both Education and Government services. They depend on the Public sector to provide the necessary Labor resources for employment in the Private sector; avoiding the major cost of Labor supply.

This shift of Tax Burden to the family households has detrimental effect upon the level of Consumption. Discretionary income is the major factor in Consumption, and the shift of Tax Burden to the Households has cut actual Discretionary Income to a probable quarter of what reinstatement of Business taxation would supply. The Reader need realize Discretionary Income stands as Marginal Income, equivalent to the Consumer, as Business Profits are to Industry; excess income over paid Expenses. The constriction of Discretionary Income levels among Consumers has been hidden by the excessive Welfare transfer payments made by Government over the last thirty years; elimination of these payments would lead to rapid reductions of Consumption, with massive Recessive constriction of the Economy. These Welfare transfer payments have consisted in the main as Social Security benefits, Housing Assistance, Child Support payments, high Personal exemptions for Dependents, PEL grants for higher Education, and public payment for Day-Care services.

Reduction of Welfare transfers could only be accomplished with the transfer of Tax Burden to Business, by implementation of equal taxation upon Business as is currently upon Households; with an almost total elimination of preferential tax credits for Business enterprise. Current Economic thought would disclaim this contention as heresy, but the Author will attempt to prove in this Work; this exact process remains the only true economic fuel left to spur the Economy. He will hopefully express what economic forces will apply, and how their interaction will bring the desired result of enhanced economic performance. Economic efficiency comes only with sharp attention to the impact of economic forces in the Economy; said operation being necessary not just for increases in Production, but for maintenance of current levels of Production. The American economy is currently sliding, and We have to reverse the trend; else We start to lose Our standard of living.

4

Elements of Consumption

Consumption exhibits all the characteristics of a all-inclusive subject, where no matter how great or extensive the analysis; half will be left unsaid. It in definition remains the use of materials in the conduct of human life. This use withdraws some degree of capacity from further use—i.e., consumption of the value of the materials. Products of the Economy divide naturally according to the loss of this value; falling into categories of Free Naturally Replaceable Goods—like Air or Water, Long-term Goods—Land and Housing for example, Medium-Term Goods—like Cars and Refrigerators, and Short-Term Goods—Food, Fuel, and most Clothing. Some Goods, most notable Electricity, are termed Immediate Use Goods; their value lasting only a short time after production. There is the story of the Ice Cube, where a Naturally-Replaceable Water requires a Medium-Term Refrigerator and Immediate-Use Electricity to generate an Ice Cube, which will melt in a half-hour without further refrigeration; expressing the necessary intermix of all Goods to produce desirable quantities.

The above story relates an important element of the Economy: Goods in the Economy may be raw resource, or processed product to add value for human consumption. Raw resource has a Price determined by the cost of recovery of the resource, itself a processing production, and the amount of the raw ore left in Nature. Water for the Ice Cube would call for pumping from a Fresh water source, not a Sewer pipe; the degree of purity is important, placing a limitation on amount of raw ore. Processed products have a price dictated by the amount of capital equipment utilized in the production of it with it's quantity of production per consumption of such equipment(potential number of Units produced, before necessary replacement of equipment or extensive Maintenance), the labor entailed in it's production, it's distribution and marketing costs, and the amount of finished product demanded by the Consuming market. The Raw resource used in the Processed Product is contained within the Capital Equipment cost, though most Economists would disagree with such a wide use of the term Capital Equipment.

All Processed Products contain some degree of Raw resource. Raw resource requires some degree of Capital Equipment for ore extraction. Human labor goes into raw resource extraction, capital equipment manufacture, processed product manufacture, and marketing and distribution of the products. Ownership of the Land from which the ore is extracted must also be paid; this payment determined by the amount of ore available, both to the Owner and to the total Economy. The interrelationship of the Economy can easily be seen, with a continual pattern of return to raw resource for additional ore with added elements of capital equipment to furnish Processed Product.

There is an innate relationship between all Products, due to the use of Capital Equipment utilized from the Ore extraction onward; not excluding the necessary human labor involved. End-line Consumer products, as generously defined by Economists, are often not End-line products at all; as they constitute products necessary for the proper provision of Labor. Employees must have Food, Shelter, Heat, Food storage, Transportation, Work clothing, and Tools. They further need Education and Training, Capital Equipment, and Materials in order to produce. Rarely is there any End-Product, except for possibly Religion.

The pricing for all Goods and Labor at every stage of the Production process becomes very important to the functioning of the total Economy. Excessive Resource pricing will raise the price of all Products. Limitation of Capital Equipment will lessen the productivity of Labor, as will a shortage of Training or Experience. The lessened amount of Product will raise the price of this product in the face of constant Consumption Demand, increasing the cost of further production of Dependent products. Reduced or insufficient Wages will lead to reduced levels of qualified Labor, and reductions of Consumption. The Blind Hand of the Market simply expresses the need for Product pricing to remain in a matrix, with some proportionality between Product prices; all this in order for the Economy to function at all.

Consumption levels remains the slave of Product pricing. Consumption can only occur with the ability to pay, and Consumption levels will fall with the addition of increased Product pricing. This can be amended by the extension of Credit, which is only an agreement of future payment for the Product with an additional payment to the Lender as Interest. This extension of Credit, though, possesses the limitation of ability of repayment. The Credit repayment process is very complicated, limited in more ways than the obvious.

Any Participant in the Economy will state Credit repayment is constrained by the amount of return to be expected from Labor, or from the Product underwritten. This stands as a simplification, without explanation of the process. Labor is dependent upon Wages for Credit extension repayment. Jobs can be lost, or the Labor hours utilized can be reduced; even without reduction of Wages, Income can be lost. Repayment from Wages suffers from another defect: the amount of necessary purchases must reduce in the future; either from the durability of Products purchased, or modification of lifestyle. The final alternative is an increase of Wage return, through Raise or increased Labor hours. Increases of Wage return suffers from a fatal flaw, if such increase causes an inflationary price increase in products which must be purchased. The Increase in Wage returns' increased financial viability can actually be canceled or reversed by Inflation, with decreased ability of Credit repayment. Profits from Product underwritten by Credit also suffers from the same flaws as Wages—Price reactions in the Market can reduce the ability to repay Credit extension. Short-term Maintenance Costs or early failure of Product life can necessitate recapitalization of Product, before the Credit repayment is complete.

Credit Extension agents find failure of Credit repayment to be rightfully horrid. They often insist on a wide cushion between the expected cost of repayment, and levels of Income of the debt assuming Party. They are careful to check previous assumed levels of Debt, and the record of repayment on such Debt. Interest rates on the Credit is raised, and levels of Credit extension lowered, as such repayment records worsens. Total assumed Debt of the Applicant is carefully examined, to insure ability to repay the Credit extended. Insufficient Income of the Applicant will always assure refusal of loan.

Monetarist policy of ease of Credit actually does relatively little to alter the above conditions, as Creditors insist on high levels of Income per Loan extension. The nature of Credit extension alters as Assumed Debt levels rise in the Economy. Interest rates on Consumer Credit increase to levels where they serve as impediment to actual Credit repayment. Short-term Goods cannot be financed by such Consumer Credit, as lack of product durability insists on product replacement before the loan can be repaid. Intermediate Goods become too expensive to purchase, as the Interest rates double or triple the initial purchase price. Credit extension slowly contracts to extension of Long-Term mortgages, which carry much lower Interest rates; but contains seeds of serious reduction of Consumption patterns—this occasioned by the high periodic payments demanded for repayment. Most Two-Income Households devote one Income to the sole purpose of Mortgage repayment, deeming the other Income should pay for all Household expenses and purchases. This leads naturally to further discussion of differentiation of Income.

Economics splits Income, especially in Personal Income, into their various types of usage.

The most consistent types used are Debt Repayment, Life Maintenance, and Discretionary Income. Income over these three usages is defined as Savings or Savings Income. Each should be explored in at least a casual manner. Debt Repayment Income is the most pressing, as Extenders of Credit have legal recourse to insist on repayment, only little affected by Bankruptcy laws; they can insist on return of Product or take possession of Property, or at least demand some return on their Capital. The Debtor thereby knows some residual element of his standard of living will be affected, if debt repayment is not made in a timely manner. This devotion of Income becomes almost mandatory, to avoid structural loss of financial position.

Life Maintenance Income likewise is highly constrained. A great proportion of Life Maintenance comes in the form of repetitious provision of essential products or services. Failure to underwrite these expenses leads to loss of Food, heat, light, and communications. It can also include loss of Housing. Many forms of Taxation are also included in the Life Maintenance Income; One does not refuse to pay Sales tax, Property tax, or Excise tax when loss of product or service is immediately entailed. Failure to underwrite Life Maintenance can bring Short-term loss of standard of living, as failure of Debt repayment brings loss of Long-term standard of living. The Personal or Business Consumer can afford neither of such type losses.

Debt Repayment and Life Maintenance Income must be considered straight Cost payment, with little flexibility or evasion of payment. They express almost no elasticity in relationship to Total Income in the Economic sense. They will be unlikely to decrease more than marginally when Total Income contracts. The only case where it does express elasticity is in a hyper-deflationary period, or with drops in Interest rates; this allowing for re-finance at reduced charge. The Former is rare, and will never effect the Cost of such charges within a year of drop in Total Income. The Latter inevitably involves an extension of debt repayment period, is likely to increase actual Debt load, and results in only marginal decreases in Cost; never significant to the levels of loss of Total Income. Both Debt Repayment and Life Maintenance are therefore considered Set Costs by the Economist.

Any loss of Total Income, or failure to increase, will impact Discretionary and Savings Income alone because of Set Costs. Many would believe Savings Income alone endures the loss of real or anticipated Income. Economic studies contradict this belief, establishing the impact on Savings Income is determined by cultural and class conditions. Many Personal Consumers, and most Business Consumers, realize decreases in Savings Income impact long-term economic financial positioning, while loss of Discretionary Income has few long-term economic consequences. Many Consumers opt for sharp reductions in Discretionary Income in the Short-term, before decision to reduce their Investment schedule by cutting Savings Income. This Effect expresses more definitely as Consumers approach Retirement Age, with losses of Labor income. There can be loss of fifty percent of Discretionary Income before reduction of Investment schedules, dependent upon cultural conditioning, Age, and recognition of class position.

The above analysis brings real impact to a discussion on Consumption. A number of factors enter into the development of Consumer Demand. The most important element is Discretionary Income, actually making up Eighty percent of such Demand. Other elemental factors of Consumer Demand is outstanding Debt load, current Interest rates, whether such Consumer Demand is for actual Consumption or further productive endeavor, and perceived need for Cash Reserves. Low Debt load will make Consumption more attractive, especially if it is for productive effort which will return a Profit. Low interest rates will make Debt assumption acceptable. or allow for re-finance on more-advantageous terms. Bad economic conditions, especially potential loss of Productive Income, incite Consumers to switch funds from Discretionary Income to Savings Income at a rapid rate; sometimes cutting Discretionary Income by thirty percent, up to periods of two years. Credit expansion, except for long-term Mortgages, can rarely expand greater than thirty percent of Discretionary Income in the Short-term, due to the difficulty of obtaining Credit, and the necessary payment of high Interest repayments on direct Consumer Debt. Further Credit expansion capacity reduces as Consumer Debt reaches high levels. Discretionary Income retains it's paramountcy in Consumer Demand, even under great ease of Credit conditions.

This Author considers all economic Recessive conditions to be caused by Consumer loss of Discretionary Income. Monetarists disagree, claiming it is loss of Credit extension; they declining to comment on the limitations to Credit expansion, or the erosion of viability of Short-term Credit expansion. Credit extension for Consumers, though, also has additional effect; added Interest charges reduce future Discretionary Income reserves. It becomes absolutely essential to examine the potential sources of loss to Consumer Discretionary Income.

The singular source of Discretionary Income to the average Consumer, whether Personal or Business, comes from Employment Income. Investment Income remains high, but only accounts for about thirty percent of total Consumer income, at any period of economic activity; and can drop seriously as proportion of the Total under a wide range of economic conditions. The Author estimates Investment Income will drop 5-6 times as rapidly as Employment Income under adverse economic conditions. The rationale for this derives from the need for a high level of Employment Income, in order to generate the Profits fueling Investment Income. Both must be fueled by a high level of Consumer Demand and Consumption.

The most profound loss of Consumption comes from loss of Employment Income. The second greatest loss of Consumption is derived by fear of loss of Employment Income, inciting reduction of Consumer Demand. The third greatest loss in Consumption comes from loss of Investment Income, bringing reductions in Investment ratios, re-capitalization, curtailment of Maintenance schedules, and Layoffs. Harsh Credit terms or high Interest rates bring the fourth highest loss. Adverse Tax policy, like high Sales tax or high Property tax on direct Consumers, accounts for the fifth greatest loss of Consumer Demand and Consumption. The last major loss, and most erosive over the long-term, consists of Employers' refusal to maintain an equity between Wage scales and Consumer Prices.

The first two factors are deeply impacted by modern American business practice, which expresses an increasing animosity to job security, in the pursuit of immediate pursuit of Profits. The spectra of 'Downsizing' propels four-fifths of the reaction inciting decrease of Consumer Demand through building Cash Reserves. The disturbance of Layoffs are equally as bad, on both Employment Income loss and the fear of it. Consumer Demand suffers terribly from both, in excess of harsh Credit terms. Business frightens off their Market, by usage of such vehicles. Other Business practices also sharply impact Consumer Demand. Refusal to fund medical insurance and pensions cause unnecessary losses of Consumer Demand, as Business can fund such needs through Group insurance far cheaper than can the individual Employee; these expenses will be funded of necessity, but Business could fund such activities at Sixty percent of the cost to either Government or Employee. Business insistence of retaining Cash Reserves at immense levels, and allowing Dividends to be reduced; also sharply reduces Consumer Investment Income. Current Business practice remains it's own worst enemy.

Monetarist policy may have created as many demons as it has eliminated. Ease of Credit terms has both beneficial and adverse effects. Credit extension brings short-term increases of standard of living, but costs long-term consequences; as Consumption is advanced through loss of Savings Income levels. Total Consumption is decreased by increased Product pricing, this due to the Interest which must be paid; a loss to Total purchasing power by a probable average of Eight percent of total purchases. Monetarist and Supply-Side concentration on Business Profits has invaded the financial markets, which now search for Returns equal to Productive activity; a most untraditional position, such activity heretofore considered ancillary to Production, with less Return but higher security. Usury laws now discarded reflected the legally-guaranteed less risk of financial instruments, and demanded limitation of demanded profits. The discard of these laws breaks the natural flow of Market forces, which all Economists pay at least lip-service to; the banking industry now violating basic traditional practice, with vastly increased risks to the entire Economy via such disasters as the S&L Bailout of the Eighties.

Supply-Side Economics insist Tax Cuts promote the Economy, though realistic proof through statistical detail has not been forthcoming. Actual indications express an real decrease in hard Capital investments in Plant and machinery. There is often evidence of 'Downsizing' to increase immediate untaxed Profits, so many Labor cadres are lost; as is business efficiency. Further correlations portray loss of high-skilled, high-paid, pensioned Employees in favor of more youthful, non-pensioned, lower-paid Labor, to increase the level of untaxed Profits; this did at marked inefficiency of business performance. There is definite loss of Consumer Demand as high-end Labor is transferred to Unemployment Benefits or low-Wage positions. The loss of Pension benefits, which is statistically observable, means a future loss of Consumer Demand; these Labor cadres reverting to a low, or Poverty-level retirement class.

This Author will claim the following analysis presented, though many unnamed Economists have been on the same train of thought; the Author simply being more vocal in protest. Budget deficits are the bane of the modern Economy. Supply-Side and Monetarist argument that Budget deficits must be analyzed as a percentage of GDP is fallacious, as it does not consider the impact of the deficits; simply implying it is similar to the debt load carried by the private Consumer in the Economy. The Government is the largest Consumer in the Economy, with stronger impact than the entire banking industry. Deficit spending on the part of Government actually shrinks the magnitude of the banking industry, curtailing it's lending capacity. The largest singular loss of financial liquidity derives from Government deficit spending. A most important point must be made, Government deficit spending is not just the Federal spending; but includes the excess spending of all three levels of Government, plus all their extended agencies whether included in their nominal budgets or not. Government deficit spending has equal impact in the Economy, irrelevant as to vestment.

The above element is not the greatest detriment to the Economy, though serious. The greatest danger in deficit spending lies in curtailment of Consumer Demand, which occurs in several ways. Government pressures the financial market to maintain low Interest rates, to fund their deficit initially; but to propel financial liquidity by increased Debt acquisition by the Private Sector. Financial institutions suffer under this scenario, as they entertain more risk and unsound venture at less return to themselves. They counter this business loss by shelving extremely high Interest rates on short-term, Consumer debt. Government and Business does not pay the appropriate Interest for their level of Debt, but it is shoved off on the small Consumer as hidden tax; such tax estimated as three percent of total volume of Consumer Debt. This total amount must be considered a complete loss of Consumer Demand, as the funds are not available to the Consumer for Consumption purposes.

Government has an even worse impact on Consumer Demand. Government does not fund it's consumption pattern in the Economy with deficit spending. Remember the Government, at all levels, is the largest Consumer in the Economy; at a magnitude which exceeds industry in actual purchases; purchases exclusive of raw productive materials. This level of consumption has incredible impact on Resource pricing, an estimated eight times the impact of Consumer consumption of End-products. Deficit spending also insists Government does not fund this competition with Private Consumers. It means Private Consumers must compete with a myth, having no economic validity in the Economic process; but gobbling up a huge proportion of Product at whatever Price demanded.

Is the impact of Government spending greater on Resource pricing, than is productive industry itself? The answer is no, if the process is funded. One may ask how this could be; the answer is relatively easy.

Funded Government spending is funded by taxation, this taxation paid by Private Consumers in the Economy. They are devoting a segment of their Income to a Good; i.e., Government spending. Resource pricing is not affected, because it means a natural decrease of Consumer Demand; the replacement of Private Consumption Goods with Public expenditure. Resource pricing will not increase unnaturally.

The Spectrum changes drastically with deficit spending, as Government refuses to fund it's competition with Private Consumers. It compels a production level of Goods which is unnaturally high, not based on normal Payment from financial extractions from the Production process itself. Many Economists would claim this is a good, as pushing for higher Production levels than normal. It actually has almost the opposite effect, with a decline of Economic performance.

The actual Cost of consumption by Government deficit spending is paid by increased Resource pricing. The actual cost of consumption must be paid, else all Productive employment would show loss of profitability; therefore, Resource prices rise as due the profits at every stage of the production process. The cost of all Consumer products, Government and Private Consumer, rise to cover the full cost of consumption from Government deficit spending. Government ignores this Consumption cost increase, simply adding to the deficit. Productive employment simply passes the cost increase on to Consumers as Price increases, added by artificially low Interest to themselves for Debt acquisition. Consumers not engaged in productive profiteering, like Business, must rely on Wage or other Income; else raise their total Debt levels.

Limitations to increased debt for Consumption purchase has already been examined, and is tied to Wage or Income return. Consumers can insist on increase in their return, demand ease of Credit extension at better terms, or reduce their Consumption; the only alternatives to the economic constrictions they face. Business is resistant to Wage Increase demands, and hires less skilled and less expensive labor whenever possible. Financial institutions show adamant refusal to reduce Interest rates, when this reduction constrains their profitability on their total operations; curtailed by Government insistence on low Interest rates for themselves and Business.

Government deficit spending, when accompanied by suppressed Interest rates for Government and Business, will always lead to a steady drop in Consumer Demand in the Private Sector, as Consumers are priced out of the Market. This drop cannot be forestalled by any initiative subject to the above conditions. The drop is predicable and equal to the total deficit spending by Government, after a three year delay. Liberalization of Interest rates for Consumer debt will have little impact on the Scenario, only increase Consumer debt to the limits permitted by financial institutions; thereby only delaying the Drop by about fourteen months in effect.

The Author knows some Readers untrained in Economics may not understand the message presented by this Chapter. The content can be put much simpler: Government deficit spending directly decreases Consumer Demand after a durative period, severely raising Product Costs from the Start, and lowers the Standard of Living of all participant Consumers. It does this by increases in Production Costs and residual Profits at every stage of Production, from Resource extraction to Marketing of End-Product Goods. The following Chapters will explore how these conditions can be avoided by elimination of Government deficit spending at all levels.

5

Taxes and What They Do.

All forget the basic limitation of any form of taxation. Tax is raised to defray the cost of Public expenditures, the only alternative being aggregation of Public Debt. This Debt must eventually be paid off by future taxation, or refinance of Debt. Public expenditure has no other functional means of Payment, except for the creation of Inflation through a mix of means; from simple printing of money to usurpation of the banking industry to pegging Wage levels of Employment and acting as Business in profit-taking. This lack of adaptability for payment of Government expenditure brings reciprocal lack of adaptability to the process of Taxation. Modern Economists since Keynes has suggested alteration of Tax Policy can bring increase in economic performance. This Chapter attempts denial of this Contention in the larger context, if not in small, isolated Event formulations.

High levels of Taxation cripple an Economy to perform; study of the historic performance of Salt monopoly economies express the highest levels of Taxation with Government acting as business. Such economies raise huge revenues for Government, but sharply curtail business expansion; while suppressing the potential standard of living to a minimum of one-half. Lesser high-tax systems express rapid lessening of Government revenues, but with slow advance of business opportunity and standards of living. All high-tax systems propel the development of a aristocracy based upon control of taxation, with all other elements suffering greater loss of standard of living; thus payment of the life-styles of the aristocracy.

High-tax systems must be eliminated before true economic performance can be attained; this economic performance consisting of several economic elements. First, all elements of society must have participation in the Economy; this meaning the elimination of Slavery, Debt Slavery, and non-transferable Poverty in a Two-Tier Economy. Second, the payment of the Means of Production must meet the conditions of Recapitalization; this meaning a profitability level equal to at least continuous replacement of capital equipment. Third, each element of Society must be able to maintain his or her own participation in the Economy; i.e., Wage/Profit/Rent levels must be sufficiently high and proportional as to maintain the lifestyles of the Participants. Fourth, Profit and Wage levels must be systematically high enough to attain Investment and Training necessary for expansion of the Economy, as to match economic performance increases to Population increases. High-tax rate systems will not allow for full exploitation of the above necessities, with withdrawal of standard-of-living until a basic Trades Society based on agriculture is reached.

Lower-Tax rate systems often do not meet all of the above conditions, though they have the capacity to do so. This failure comes from misplacement of Tax assessment to exploit the above conditions. Tax systems, therefore, reflect more danger to economic performance than they have reflected potentiality for stimulus of the Economy. The Author will here claim the sole economic stimulus exhibited by Tax Policy comes in the form of elimination of Tax Assessment misplacement. There is much denial of this View, most dissension coming from Economic elements who would actually increase the misplacement of Tax Assessment.

Tax, in the Short-Run or in a Interest-costing Long-Run, must pay for Government expenditure. Accumulation of Public Debt, as analyzed in the pervious Chapter, is actually harmful to Economic performance. This impels payment of Government expenditures in the immediate Period, as they are incurred. Conservative Economists would call for reduction of Government expenditure under these conditions, but Government expenditures are often necessary for maximization of Economic performance. Excessive tax rates retard the Economy, so increased Government expenditures must be paid for by gradually increased tax rates, which possess the least impact on the Economy. This is nothing but the definition of proper Tax placement.

Government must provide Infrastructure for the furtherance of business performance—Roads, Bridges, Communications, etc. Government must provide some milieu for the training of Labor cadres, else there is a drop of productivity; Business able to develop 'directed-end' training alone, utilizing Labor resources with previously-provided educational training. Governments must provide Law Enforcement for protection of Property rights and Individual safety. Government must also provide a medium for Conflict Resolution between economic participants—the basic for Tort law. Government must also promote and regulate Safety in the Workplace, otherwise unlimited practice brings falling rates of production; this including Environmental pollution standard, Product standards, and Building Codes. These remain functional irreducible Costs of Government expenditure, and actually constitute Sixty-five percent of Government cost; when viewing all three levels of American governments.

The above-mentioned Government Costs are heavily labor-intensive and capital-intensive, as well as being irreducible. Total Economic cost of these Services by Government functionally could not be minimized below Eight percent of GDP, and probably could not be reduced below Twelve percent of GDP without serious loss of economic performance. Reduction of funding of such activities would simply incur a hidden tax of decreased Economic performance. Conservatives who would tamper with these Costs, tamper with their own standard of living. Interaction with the above analysis produces a necessity for a Tax base revenue withdrawal of at least Twelve percent of the GDP—Gross Domestic Product to the Layperson.

A Minima of Tax Revenue Generation has been established by the Analysis, which the Author contends must be expanded for peak economic performance. Some level of Communal Medical Service must be provided, in order for economic Participants to remain active in the Economy. Private insurance does not, and cannot, serve all; though the medical service must be basically universal to a minimum level. Underwriting of the children of the Poor to an extent they can attain the participatory skills necessary for economic labor is a must. The lack of welfare-transfer payments will lead to sharp curtailment to participation by many segments of Society in the Economy. This Last should not be contested by Conservatives; Social Security and Medicare must be considered Welfare-transfers, as they are not funded by Beneficiaries in actuality, and these payments are the most lucrative payments in the Welfare-transfer system. Participation by the Elderly would decrease a minimum of thirty percent without these payments. Real drops in GDP would be incurred without this funding. The real cost of these services require a probable minimum of Four percent of GDP, bringing the actual Minima of Tax Revenue Generation to a level of Sixteen percent of the GDP of a modern Economy.

A turn will now be made to the potentiality of using Tax Policy as economic stimulus. Analysis has established the paramountcy of Tax Collections equal to Government Expenditures, in order to fund Government competition with Private Consumers; all this to prevent drops of Consumer Demand greater than simple reduction by Public consumption of Goods. Tax initiatives which reduce the necessary Tax revenues below Government Expenditures create greater Economic performance reduction, than they could promote. Tax Policy initiatives for economic stimulus must maintain necessary Tax revenues, so such initiatives devolve into alternate placement of Tax Assessment. The proper placement of Tax assessments compose the majority of Chapters in the rest of this Book.

Greater examination of Government Expenditures must be made, before We turn to the arena of Tax assessments. Government remains the greatest Consumer in the modern economy. It's composition as a Consumer, though, also holds an equal relevance. The Government is the sole Consumer for a vast range of Products and Services. These are generated by specialized industries, who could not continue without Government purchases. Industries supplying Ports, Airports, Military Bases, and even National Parks would not exist without regular Government payments. Most of these industries are not totally devoted to Government supply, but sell many Goods to the Private Sector; without being able to do so, without Government purchase of the majority of their Product. They could not survive as a Provider to only the Private Sector, as Capital Costs exceed Recapitalization and Profitability rates of such supply, due to insufficient demand by the Private Sector. Loss of Government purchase functionally killed the Shipbuilding industry of the United States. Many other American industries and businesses would follow American Shipbuilding into history, without extensive Government purchases.

Government needs fund almost half the Research conducted in the Country, which would be eliminated by a reduction of Government investment and purchase. Government needs brought the Private Sector everything from modern Tires to Tang. Government funds much of the Research done by academic institutions. Government funding of medical research exceeds the Drug industry. Cancellation of such Research would deeply impact the American standard of living. Government funding of Agricultural research has doubled agricultural output, providing Our most prominent export while feeding the American population. Government research studies have probably increased the efficiency of Private Sector production methods by Ten to Twelve percent alone. Road Safety Research Studies have probably saved 100,000 American lives and Five Billions dollars worth of Property damage per year. These are all activities which Private industry could not profitably have funded.

Government purchase at all three levels does much to insure the profitability of many industries, who mostly supply the Private Sector.

Government purchase of Light bulbs undoubtedly exceeds Household consumption. Government may purchase more Concrete than the Private Sector. Government's Telephone Bill probably exceeds the total of all Household bills, competing seriously with American business. Government Employees never shut off the lights, so the electric bill is high. Even Government purchase of Garden equipment—especially Lawn—rivals private Households. The impact of Government is huge.

The total bill of Government can be discounted with Infrastructure Use costs being assessed. Airport passenger and commercial use can be attributed to cost about $1.27 per usage unit, this high only due to maintenance and recapitalization upgrades. Amtrack per unit costs would be extremely cheap, except for the lack of routes and delays of arrival; Studies indicate such travel could be multiplied by a factor of Six, if these elements were corrected. Such a rate of usage would easily capitalize the whole system at a Profit. The rate of unit travel on the Highway system expresses mere Pennies per unit cost. The addition of Infrastructure may be the cheapest capital increment in the Country.

Actual simple Law Enforcement is a Labor-intensive industry. It must be attributed to be very expensive, but Cost analysis expresses not a serious cost. Actual number of Site calls and Police response on a daily basis indicate rates much cheaper than calling a Plumber, or having your Lawn mowed. The greatest Cost associated at per unit Cost level in Law Enforcement comes in the form of supporting the Judicial system, where almost all Officials and Employees enjoy extraordinary Payscales, with extremely low daily unit handling. Usage of Court decisions to determine Work schedules, plus the supply of Legal aid to the Indigent, suppress the rate of determinations to where per unit cost exceeds $4000 per unit. This competes with a probable per unit cost for actual Law Enforcement of less than $30. The Readers should realize where Government costs arise, and from what source.

Medical Response Units and Emergency Rooms are a incredibly expensive item for Governments, but unit cost analysis provides great insight into the Problem. Labor per unit response rate probably does not exceed $30 per unit call for Ambulance teams. Labor per unit cost rate for Emergency Room use probably does not exceed $180 per unit usage, even with the addition of Doctors' pay. A simple Ambulance unit without equipment probably costs no more than $65,000 per unit, the use of 'probably' due to the erratic nature of price increases in the entire medical supply industry. Outfitting an Ambulance with full medical capability triples the vehicle cost. Emergency Room medical outfitting can carry a Price tag over $5 million.

The outfitting for medical capability needs to be explored. Medicines which can be produced as cheaply as Aspirin sold in a Drugstore, cost in excess of $20 per pill when administered by hospital staff. Computerized IV drip units carry Price tags in excess of $4000 in many instances, when more precise units are provided to Business applications for production at less than $500 per unit. Much medical machine applications are provides at per-Unit costs in excess of $30,000 per unit, where more precise machine applications are provided for industrial production at per-Unit rates of less than $5000. Great amounts of medical materials (gloves, gowns, Needles, syringes, etc.) come at Prices often 6000 percent over costs charged to industry production equivalent products; these with standards often in excess of what is demanded for medical materials. Supply of medical services by Government is not an unacceptable cost to the Taxpayers, though purchase of supplies for these medical services from a usurious medical supply industry most certainly is impossible to maintain. An unofficial study sought to provide full equipage of an Ambulance at industrial production purchase rates; the total impact of that Cost, above the cost of the vehicle, was $14,000.

Housing subsidies and Welfare transfers are a major irritant to Conservatives. They rant and rage against such wealth transfer. Actual economic impact may show they are somewhat foolhardy in their outrage. The Author estimates total Rent rates for Housing would drop nationwide by some 11%, if all Housing subsidies were stopped. This means Landlords would lose one-tenth of their Income, if Taxpayers did not pay the Rent for some Eight percent of the American population. Welfare transfers account for approximately Six percent of all purchases of Groceries in the Country, and almost One percent of all Clothing; this only if Social Security benefits are not considered Welfare transfers. The rates would be 18% of Groceries, and 11% of the Clothing purchases; if and when Social Security benefits are considered Welfare transfers. The Above indicates Grocers and Retailers would lose a significant amount of Profits from Sales, and Landlords would lose drastically with the loss of Social Security benefits paid. Social welfare is not an unacceptable cost, when considering the loss of standard of living and Business profits.

Examination of Government expenditures expresses a glaring fact to the Economist. Labor Costs for Government are extremely high, but probably not glaringly greater than Labor Costs to Private industry. Government must be considered a Labor-intensive industry, where Labor rolls could not be significantly reduced in face of the level of programs; though it is undoubted Americans could live with only half of the Civil Service and programs of Government. Welfare recipients made only a small cost to Government, if the Social Security program is excluded from the matrix. Their major cost comes from purchases from a bloated-Profits medical supply industry. Budget delineation analysis clearly portrays the fact American tax dollars turn into Business Profits, at rates which are extreme; total Profits probably exceeding by a factor of 3 to 8 times total benefits paid for social programs, even with the inclusion of Social Security.

The Author would like to state the equation clearly: Government expenditures are Welfare transfers, but the transfers are made from American Taxpayers to Business Profits. Analysis of the cost of actually supporting all Recipients of Government support, when subtracting all Profits to Business but including Government Employee labor costs, devolves into a cost of less than one-tenth of the current Budget. (The parameters of the Hypothesis does not include Medicare and Social Security benefits, stipulate Government labor costs do not exceed the level exhibiting in the Private Sector, and the costs of Goods bought by Recipients were purchased at only a Eight percent profit for Manufacturers). The Author is not an opponent to Capitalism or Business Profits, but remains an advocate for Government Bargaining procedures in-line with procedures exercised by Private industry. Adoption of such rules would halve the cost of Government in this Country.

6
Types of Taxes

The Author has already a Work, FORMS OF TAXATION (iUniverse, 2002), dealing with the various kinds of Taxes which have been developed. This Chapter will hopefully not be a repetition of the previous labor. He would herein attempt to develop the conceptional organization of Taxes. Taxes are designed to get popular subscription of Government expenses; i.e., to get the People to pay for what political leadership wishes to spend. Statistical Polls have never been taken, but sentiment would indicate the majority of Taxpayers would reject almost any placement of Tax if they could. The Author suggest no placement of any Tax has more support than twenty percent of the Population, and almost sixty percent of the Populace would actively support a real reduction of the impact of the specific Tax. All Citizens realize a need to pay for Government expenditure, but this expense should be borne in greater proportion by Others than themselves. It is the heavy impact of Self-Interest in Tax placement, and a major detriment to judicious distribution; as Taxpayers gain political lobbyist organizations.

Taxes can be placed on almost any item, which can be individualized in some process. They have been placed on Individuals as a Head Tax; if you are here, you are taxed. This can be radicalized, as a heavy Birth Tax has occasionally been placed on Fathers; still present in American society to a slight degree, as Child Support payments upon divorce. Most Single Mothers could be outraged at this analysis, but there is an Argument that the Child should be overjoyed to have been brought to life; neither he, his mother, or the State should be so ungrateful as to demand more. The Author, by the way, does not ascribe to this Argument; bowing to the general Consensus of family life.

The Head Tax proved unworkable. The Tax had to be low, so even the economically menial elements of Society could pay. This caused and acute shortage in the revenues collected from the Tax. There was always dispute over who should pay for the Old and Young, who did not have the wherewithal to pay. Transfer of the Tax to only the Working population vastly cut the revenues, due to reduced Rolls and the necessary low payment; to account for the low-Wage workers. The basic groundwork for a graduated Income tax had been laid.

Many Conservatives proclaim the advantages of a Flat Tax, or a set-percentage Income tax. It remains a puerile suggestion because of ramifications. It insists Lower Incomes have the same ability to pay, as do Higher-Income classes; totally ignoring the betterment of position derived by aggregation of capital resources. The regressive aspects of such taxation is not really the Issue with the Flat Tax. The real adverse impact comes in an accelerating advantage for the Higher-Income classes to pay the set-rate, while Lower-Incomes lose ability to maintain the same revenue level of payments. The Poor begin to pay less and less tax, Middle-range Incomes begin to join the Poor, and total revenues begin to drop. The Government comes under pressure to increase the rate of tax to pay for expenses. The Author states here that many Economists disagree with this analysis, though they refuse to quantify the advantage of capital aggregation.

The Graduated Income Tax is not a panacea altogether, as it becomes a medium of political lobbyist activity. Lower-Incomes unite in demands for high tax rates to be assigned to the Wealthy. The Wealthy possess the financial resources for heavy lobbyist efforts, profitable up to the total value of the tax assessment. Political lobbyists and Politicians quickly learn not to directly challenge the greater Mass of

Lower-Incomes; and so high tax rates stay, but the reign of legal tax evasion is borne, better known as the Age of Exemptions from Tax.

Tax exemptions come with all the names of the Rainbow; called Personal Deductions, Dependent Deductions, Mortgage exemptions, Medical Expense deductions, Investment credits, Business organization deductions, recapitalization exemptions, tax credits, Employee credits, Delayed Investment credits, IRA accounts, 401K accounts, Elderly deferment exemptions, Grandfather clause exemptions, and Balance Forward exemptions. They all mean the same: the ability to avoid paying tax legally; all built by political lobbyist effort; residing in a totally obtuse Tax Code, never read except by Tax Account lawyers and CPAs; they using the language to save their Clients from paying taxes. Economists also develop their own terminology to analyze the tax procedures: describing the nominal tax versus the real or actual tax, doing the same for discussion of tax rates.

Readers should be able to discern the difference between nominal and real tax, or nominal and real tax rate. Wealthy Individuals or Business Entities often will be assessed a nominal tax of some several millions of dollars; often paying a real tax of some few thousands of dollars. The nominal tax rate might be 40% or more on higher Incomes, but real tax rate percentage of actual taxes paid to Income might be as low as Two percent of the Gross before the impact of tax exemptions. The Author remembers of the honesty of a President, who claimed he and his wife made several hundreds of thousands of dollars, paying some $14,000 as tax; though he did not have to, because of legal exemptions he could have taken. The President was Bill Clinton, not the greatest Pillar of Honesty in American society; so One can understand the feeling of safety the Wealthy enjoy in this system of legal tax evasion. Our latest President gave Tax Rebates to Corporations, who had not paid the Taxes in the first place; the funds coming from the very regressive tax on Lower-Incomes, who cannot exercise the tax exemption evasion due to lack of financial magnitude. The entire Process turns a Graduated Income Tax into a sharply regressive tax system, where the Wealthy pay little and Medium-Incomes pay almost all taxes.

The Middle-Incomes Classes seem like they should be able to express a high degree of political acumen; sufficient to overturn this sharply-skewed tax schedule. The political process nullifies this participation of the Middle-Incomes. It first confuses all of Society, especially the Middle-Incomes, so they themselves support the regressive tax. Lobbyists tie the Investment schedules of Middle-Incomes to the wealth of High-Income classes. This is done by imposition of a flat tax on Capital Gains, which will not tax upon degree of success; so Billionaires pay the same approximate rate as Middle-Incomes. They then present only Open-End exemptions, telling Middle-Incomes they can only get their $2000 per year tax remissions; if and only if, Upper Incomes can gain their $30-40 Million a year tax remissions. The political interests negate the power of protest from Middle-Incomes further, by removing the Poor from taxation, and threatening need to withdraw funds from the Social Security; which propels the Gray Generation to support current tax measures. Throughout the Process of support generation for tax evasion for the Wealthy, the Political Machine proclaimed loss of economic performance if Business is overtaxed.

The Lowest-Incomes and Social Security recipients all believe they benefit from the placement of the burden of tax upon the Middle-Incomes. This could not be further from the case. The taxation of the Lower-Incomes has simply been transferred to other forms of tax. Working Poor actually support half of the Social Security burden, in comparison to half of a percent of the burden by the top One Percent of Taxpayers. These One-Percenters are actually four times as likely to use the full benefits of Social Security and Medicare, than are Recipients who were originally from the Working Poor—all because of the need for matching funds introduced by Politicians intent on cutting the cost of the programs; this fully and directly intent on cutting out benefits to the Poor. The cost of Social Security tax for the Working

Poor has come to rival the cost of the Income tax of some decades ago. Social Security beneficiaries do not benefit from this process, as they meet ever-increasing matching funds to draw Medicare benefits. A continual revolving 'Basket of Goods' to determine the rate of Inflation allows Government to reduce the impact of COLAs (Cost of Living Advances) to approximately two-thirds of actual Inflation.

Lower Incomes may believe they are at least only being charged the same rate of tax as in previous years. They could not be more wrong. The Wealthy and Politicians have worked strenuously to reduce their tax burden, shifting it onto the Poor. A prime case in point comes in the study of the progress of Property taxation in this Country. Business enterprise is allowed a multitude of exemptions from the impact of Property tax. This factor alone can be expected to have caused a 6-8% Nationwide Property tax increase, this is a real percentage increase of taxation; not a nominal simple increase in Inflation.

The Federal Government has been shifting the cost of Road Construction to the States, where it is shifted to Property tax, Sales taxes, and Personal Income taxes. Politicians at the State Level work hard to shift this Cost to Sales and Property taxes, off Personal Income taxation. This process factor can be estimated to have caused a real Property tax increase of approximately 34%, and a real Sales tax increase of almost 50%. Shift of Unemployment Benefits, Medicaid benefits, Housing Assistance, and Child Support benefits to the State level from previous Federal payment, can be expected to have caused a real tax increase in Property tax of twenty percent, a real increase in Sales tax of thirty percent, and a real increase in State Income tax of fourteen percent. Many would exclaim this could not be true, but where did the Sales tax of Two percent go to? What happened to the House Property tax of $300 of a couple decades ago? The average Property tax on a Four-Bedroom house will exceed $4000 per year before 2005. The increase in State Income taxes has averaged only about half the Inflation rate.

The Reader probably thinks this Chapter should have been named 'Tax Impact' at this point, but the Author still needs to amplify the various types of taxes, what they are designed to fund and pay for, and the Designers' intent of where the burden of the tax should fall. Beginning students of taxation must understand Politicians do not mistakenly impact the wrong Polity with a tax. Taxes are designed with specific intent, and Tax systems are altered through Political lobby to shift the tax burden off those who fund the Lobby. The shift of the tax burden from Wealthy elements onto the Poor was consciously designed, and implemented by generous contributions to Politicians. There is remarked little good will in the Process.

The Graduated Income Tax was originally designed for the purpose collecting shortfalls in Government revenue, not being covered by Imposts and Tariffs. The magnitude of tax was not expected to be large at the time of it's implementation; functionally, it was supposed to raise a percentage revenue equal to the current Sales tax levels. The provisions for Graduation of taxation according to ability to pay was thought as just and financially viable. The Era of Big Government intervened, and brought huge increases to the tax rates applied. Special Interests took up the Cause of tax remission, funded with potential to be saved by those remissions. Study of the tax system quickly identified several considerations.

The most vital consideration apparent to All concerned the need to fund Government expenditures. The total revenue generation from the Income Tax could not actually decrease substantially, as Deficits would be astronomical without ability for even servicing the Debt incited. It was immediately recognized any tax remission for the Wealthy must come by shift of the tax burden to lower Income classes. The principle of tax fairness was a rapid victim of the Process, as the politically powerful refused to surrender their desire for tax remission. The real decisive change in political motivation for Tax alteration came with the Kennedy Tax Cut of the early Sixties of the last Century. Lawmakers surrendered the principles of general tax formulation, for the more politically expedient special dispensations.

Great inroads of erosion into tax collection have been accomplished since that time. Business and Wealthy classes use political lobbies to amend tax legislation to benefit themselves at every level. Property tax has been rerouted by 'Free Enterprise Zones', designations of Commercial and Residential zones, and the Evaluation process. Business uses every means to evade local taxation, while the Wealthy do not pay Property tax at the same multiple of the value of their Property to that of poorer Properties. Sales tax pervades every Consumer product, but does not touch Business needs. Federal taxation, with the latter Bush brand of taxation, holds absolutely no threat of loss to Corporations; along with little loss for other forms of Business.

There are several suggested forms for elimination of the Inheritance tax. Readers should realize these changes are only for the benefit of the very Wealthy, as normal heirs face little impact from the Inheritance tax, due to the mildness of taxation in the lower ranks. Elimination of the Inheritance tax is not really the necessary discussion here, though the Author believes in elimination of aristocracies through heavy transference taxation between Generations. The issue of note lies in the proposed legislation, which all contain provisions for evasion of normal Income tax. Current Tax law allows for deferment of taxation if registered for Retirement or Investment. The proposed Inheritance tax bills all allow for continuance of this deferment through the lifetime of the Original Holder unto his heirs. The effect of these Proposals signify ability to limit payment of tax only to the amount of funds actually spent any given year, with no taxation of the Principal at any time. It, in effect, would allow for the 'Grandfathering' of Wealth down through the Ages; with only a small taxation on the Interest spend. Those still working for a Living would still have to pay the tax, but the Wealthy would only have to pay a small percentage of their living expenses.

Types of Taxes can only be defined by their impact under the current profligate usage of all forms of tax exemptions; the Author could literally not define all separate delineation names for them, he would undoubtedly miss half of the names. They have been generated for the last four decades, with the express purpose of allowing tax evasion for Business and Wealthy. Working Taxpayers must realize the Process, before they can fight it. Readers may ask why they should fight this Trend. Many answers could be given, but the Author enjoys use of a favorite of his: All the personal exemptions and deductions allowed to working Taxpayers making less than $100,000 per year, could not equal twenty percent of the Savings granted to Corporations, other Business interests, and the Wealthy by these special dispensations from all three levels of Government. Introduction a general, uniform Tax Code applicable upon All could lower the real tax rate for working Taxpayers; while eliminating the National Debt and Deficits at all three levels, a real Positive in impact on the Economy as noted earlier.

7

General Forms of Taxation

The general forms of taxation used by the United States has been Property, Sales, Income, Excise, Ta riffs, and Imposts on Documents. There is a wide range of named taxes, but almost all will fall beneath the above designations. Property is split between Residential and Commercial, as well as being generated in different tax jurisdictions. Sales taxes are limited almost universally to Consumer Goods. Income tax is understood by Anyone who works, but contains so many deviations from the norm; no One could pay the stipulated rate of taxation. Excise taxes are gathered on specific Goods, often with intent to distract from their usage; most Economists insist these taxes are minor Today, totally ignoring Gas and Cigarette Excises from such deliberation. Tariffs are condemned by the Economic profession Today, who insist such usage diminishes from economic performance; you will learn later this Author disagrees with the general sentiment. Imposts on Documents should be a minor item, but isn't; consider getting a laminated $.30 piece of paper with $.60 picture overshadowed as Driver's License, for a general fee of $15.

The Author uses a strict interpretation of the United States Constitution to adjudge legality. He does signify the Constitution grants the right to regulate the Economy to the Federal government. He is called a Radical for the belief this grants the Federal legislative branch the right to set all Tax rates in the Nation, in the interest of alignment of economic performance. Almost all Others see a Constitutional conflict with this Position. The end-fact remains such uniform taxation would be the best economic performance factor available.

Uniform tax rates in this Country perform on many levels, almost all beneficial. The multiplicity of tax impact would be eliminated, so transfer of Commercial effort would not be paid by Government exemption. Empowerment Zones and Free Enterprise Zones would become a thing of the past, demanding Business share in the payment for Community services. Actual Recapitalization rates would go up, as physical transfer of Plant became more expensive. Interaction between Business and Community would increase, with Businessmen on Town Councils for purposes other than tax evasion. Simplicity of tax payment would be gained, as payment had to be sent only to the proper jurisdiction, without complications of tax rate determinations.

The importance of this Change means far more than the Above. The greatest benefit lay in the imposition of a low tax rate upon All. The Author believes the proper Property tax rate across the United States should be One percent of the Equity, for all Property—Residential and Commercial. Actual outcome of imposition of such a rate would bring an actual increase of tax revenues in almost every tax jurisdiction, force usage or Sale of all Properties, reduce actual tax impact upon residential properties, and curtail the ability of subordinate Government entities to finance by deficit spending. The last caused by financial institutions' recognition of restricted repayment schedules for subordinate Governments.

Most Sales taxes are unrealistically high, as they curtail Consumption faster than the rate of revenue generation. There is a point determined by Price/Quantity schedules intersection where increased Sales tax rates actually reduce Sales to the point less revenue is generated. Economists would say this is not really true, as Sales tax rate percentages are so low; long-term diminution does not occur. It is in the long-term where the reduction of Sales occurs to the point where the reduction occurs. It is not the initial payment of Sales tax which impacts, it is the long-term impact on the Purchase decision of the continuing loss of revenue from such taxation; which reduces Consumer Demand. Technically put (at which the Author is poorly adapted), it is comparison of the Limits of the various Marginal Utilities exhibited in the Third-Generation of Purchase Utility decisions where the falling off is found. It is better expressed in human terms as only 77% likelihood of purchase of a Good, after having paid high Sales taxes on a number of previous purchases of that specific Good. The Consumer opts for doing without, or purchase of a cheaper Substitute Good some 23% of the time. The effect on Substitute Goods will be the same by the Third Generation of Purchase decisions. The Layman will be better informed by statement there is a continuous decline in the standard of living, under the impact of excessive Sales tax rates.

The exact point of excess for a Sales tax rate finds much contention. Most Economists refuse to recognize any detriment to Consumer Demand. Many Economists believe there should be no Sales tax at all, among those who witness the hazard. Certain studies indicate a maximum of 4.3% Sales tax rate stands as the decisive point, where Third Generation Purchase decisions begin a decisive slide below a Ten percent decrease. The Author believes any Sales tax rate higher than Three percent represents a risk, accelerating declines in Consumer Demand faster than simple percentage increases. Explanation of Third Generation Purchase decisions should be made at this point. They are a complicated formulation even for Economists. They are basically the round of purchase decisions made by the original purchaser, after the first purchases have been made, the Producers have received their Production Profits, purchased their Consumption under the impact of the Sales tax, and increased their Product prices to account for the impact of the Sales tax. The impact of the Sales tax, along with the Product price increase, determines the total impact upon Consumer Demand. The majority of Economists refuse to heed such data, insisting on considering Sales taxes as simple Production costs to the Consumer.

The problem in assigning Sales taxes to simple production costs lies Sales tax rates being laid on the final Consumer Retail price. The added

Cost increase is a percentage increase on not just Production Costs, but also on Production, Distribution, and Retail Costs and Profits. This makes the Sales tax rate a multiplier of all previous Costs and Profits. A simple statement for the Layman would be the Sales tax is also a tax upon the Profits of Production, Distribution, and Retail. A 4.3% Sales tax rate is not a simple increase in Production Costs, but an increase in the combined Profits; one which will incorporate into the future combined Profits of Production, Distribution, and Retailing after the Second Generation of Purchase decisions. This can actually raise the Consumer Price for a Product in the Third Generation above 14% over the initial price of the Product before taxation. The Fifth Generation of Purchases decisions will repeat the above process, and continue with repetitive Generations; this all without any actual increase in Production Costs, which will be increased due to Resource price increases from the Second Generation of Purchase decisions.

State Income taxes Today are based mostly on a percentage of the actual amount paid as Federal income tax, to avoid the complications of accounting various exemptions for the individual Taxpayers. This simplifies the Collection process for the States, and is probably the best solution for both State and Taxpayer. Some local Communities are also adopting such a program. The tax system formed is viable, but the rates used and the distribution of funds from the various tax systems are faulty. Some State Income tax rates are quite high, some local Community income tax rates stand as excessive. A general Tax law issued by Congress and President could be quite beneficial, if it set specific, designated Income tax rates.

The Author does not propose to stipulate specific rates, without detailed Economic studies suggesting proper assignment of funds. He does comment on the alignment. Local and County jurisdictions should receive approximately Twenty percent of the total proceeds, as they primary Community service Providers; needing a revenue base to pay for ever-increasing Costs. States should get approximately Ten percent of the total proceeds, relatively sufficient to provide for Infrastructure costs and State functions. The Federal Government would receive the remainder of the total Proceeds.

The importance of general set tax rates for Property, Sales, Inheritance, and Income tax rates soon become evident. Property, Sales, and Inheritance could not be utilized by local tax jurisdictions to fund excessive funding. The Federal Government, additionally, would have to reorganize the Personal Income tax rates in order to generate the level of total revenues; pressured by all Government entities. The inequities of the complex tax exemption system would soon fail, as Shortfalls would be immediately apparent to All. Most Lobbyist efforts to reduce specific tax burdens would be defeated under the impact of needed revenue generation. Persistent efforts would reintroduce the Concept of Fairness into the general tax base.

A short aside should be made to study Tariffs at this point. Such imposts have traditionally been assigned to specific Products, and Economists have roundly condemned them as essential restraint of Trade. Tariffs, though, are like most Economic initiatives; they are not intrinsically evil, only much abused in implementation. A general Tariff should be imposed on all Imports, with a low tax rate like Sales tax rates—the Author suggests Three percent. The very multiplier effect discussed under Sales tax rates again gains importance; this time as advantage to the Economy. Third Generation Purchase decisions would curtail uninhibited Import purchase, due to switch to domestic Substitute Goods. Economists will claim this is restraint of trade, but it really is not; technological and location advantages of Production will still be recognized, and the low tax rate would not allow domestic industry access to protective decay. It would actually impel domestic industry to upgrade to an appealing position as Substitute Goods. The moderate growth of domestic industry income propelling this upgrade would also generate expansion into foreign markets, advancing economic position in the World Economy. The revenue generated from such a tax would be significant, and help contain the expanding Infrastructure costs of the Country.

The current Administration proposes to eliminate the Capital-Gains Tax, claiming this Tax is some manner of double taxation. This Precis is stupid; the Author could lay like claim against paying Sales or Property tax, as Income tax has already been paid. The Reality states a Corporation is a distinct, separate economic entity; with Stockholders sharing this same distinct, separate economic reality. Corporations pay the Corporate Income tax on Profits they have made, because this is a real Income. Stockholder dividends are differentiated Interest which the Corporation owes to Stockholders for the differentiated Debt held by those Stockholders. In both cases, for Corporation and Stockholders, it is separate, gainful Income for each. The Author agrees Capital Gains Taxation should be eliminated, but only by the expedient of declaring Capital Gains to be Personal Income for the Recipients; with proper taxation under normal Income schedules for such Income.

Some Economists would disclaim the above Procedure as inimical to the Capital Aggregation Function. Their basic contention protests Capital Gains must have preferential Tax rates to normal Personal Income, so Investors will be inspired to devote their funds to such purpose. This accepts the implication lower rates of Taxation will induce Consumers to restrict Consumption, to enjoy a lesser taxation on future Proceeds. The Author contests this proposition, stating Individual desires for capital aggregation resides in individual desire to improve economic position; this desire fueled by gains of personal entertainment and less vigorous work schedules. Almost all of Individual drive for capital aggregation concerns a very real need for economic safety, as cushion from misfortune. Promise of lower taxation does not enter these two functions, until after extensive capital aggregation has been attained; then only to improve economic viability by discrimination against less fortunate economic Participants. The actual Capital Aggregation already exists because the Funds exist, simply in Personal Income accounts, financial institutions, or Government Treasuries. Viable economic enterprise will always be funded because of this Capital Aggregation, whether by Incorporation, financial instruments, or acquisition of Debt.

Elimination of Capital Gains would be only for the benefit of Wealthy interests, not economic performance. Actual performance evaluation suggests Corporate Internal Finance of Production actually suffers from lack of research into Production Cost and Marketing Cost schedules, bringing unprofitable Production projects; all leading to actual real losses of Capital profitability. The behavior of Stockholders suggests high returns on Investment markedly impede economic performance, as these Individuals abandon gainful labor. There is a heavy element among Stockholders of separation of economic position improvements from Individual performance, creating a Parasitic class of both themselves and their descendants. Elimination of Capital Gains taxation of any type would simply worsen the situation.

The above paragraph leads naturally to criticism of the Inheritance laws of the United States. States generally charge real Inheritance taxes higher than does the Federal Government. These rates of taxation vary greatly by jurisdiction, though, so the Wealthy exercise their ability to file Probate at most advantageous location. A uniform Federal law on Inheritance taxation need be implemented, with set tax rates split between Federal, State, and Local jurisdictions. This spreads the burden on Probate Courts evenly, eliminating the value of artificial transference. It goes further by providing a even distribution of tax revenue derived between the various levels of Government. This even spread of revenue will lead to common rules of Probate activity, an incredible benefit to heirs; who will be able to acquire understanding of what Probate lawyers are charging so highly to do. The proper distribution will also turn Inheritance taxation into a correct tax revenue system, requiring less taxation of the Living.

Inheritance tax rates need be explored for any discussion to gain pertinency. The Author believes any Parent should be able to leave his progeny in a successful position, and Family enterprise should be allowed to transfer without undue Debt. He does not believe actual economic power should be transferred from the hands which developed it, into hands which mostly are untrained for it and incompetent. A systemic program to attain the above ends stands as hard to define. It will have to be defined in order for proper Inheritance tax rates to be imposed.

A realistic proposal for Inheritance tax rates would be nothing up to One million dollars, twenty-five percent from One to Ten million dollars, and advancing percentage until the tax rate is 100% over Twenty million dollars. The trouble with such statement comes in the impact of Inflation on any numbers, and the impact on functioning business. The numbers are so large as to make the impact of Inflation minor in the short-run, with only updates potentially every decade. Economic reality suggests any business over Ten million dollars in value should be incorporated, so Inheritance law should necessitate incorporation, with use of fund-raising by going Public; this has the benefit of distributing the economic power of control of the Enterprise. It allows for the continuation of business operation with funding, and lessens the impact of Control transfer.

The central thesis of this Chapter declares the need for uniformity of tax rates for this Country. The lack of uniformity provides much injustice, provides avenue for widespread abuse, and sharply reduces tax revenue and tax viability. Uniformity of tax rates would also organize the disparate tax systems in this Nation, into a Collective system of tax; this due to the need to insure overall revenue generation. The various taxes—Property, Sales, Inheritance, Income, Corporate Income, etc., would fall into a natural alignment with each other; an alignment based upon the minimum economic impact necessary to generate the necessary revenue. The Author estimates three-quarters of adverse economic impact from taxation could be eliminated. Government Debt load at all three levels of Government would be much reduced, as necessary coordination of expenditures would be made between the three levels. The final great benefit of such coordination would be minimization of Pork Barrel projects, as alternate projects would be increasingly attractive because of their need; all under the focus of a common source of funding. The excesses of Government performance could be better controlled, with less end-cost to the American Polity.

8

Impact of Taxes

The hardest part of the Study of Taxes belongs to the arena of tax impact. Every Economist understand the heavy effect Taxation has on the normal interaction of economic processes, but They deal with the largest and most complex laboratory in existence. The disparate elements composing any economic decision are so vast, not even the specific decision-maker could catalogue the selection process. All Participants in a Economy, whether Free Market or Command, depend on pricing of Products to determine their choices. Needs are met by confrontation with such Prices, within the context of a allowable budget. Study of Tax impact is the study of what Taxes, or a specific tax, does to the Product pricing it affects. It therefore entails a previous lengthy study of the manner in which these Product prices are formed. Then formulations must be derived specifying what Product prices are affected; this propels need to devise a schedule of probable Price impacts, as all Product pricing will be affected, but most Products will not be impacted to any major degree. Other Products will endure massive price impact from a specific tax; almost all Products heavily impacted by some specific tax, but not primarily by others.

Property Tax may be the easiest tax to access, as it is a major-ticket item (ranking alongside Mortgage and Food as major expense). It's impact on Consumer Demand is a function of the percentage of total real taxation to the total Income of the Property-holder. Consumer Demand, though, can be much more massive impacted than this simple percentage, due to subtraction of inflexible Costs (like Mortgage payments, Utilities, etc.) from the total Income of the Property owner. Thus the actual cost of Property tax is the total percentage of real payment of tax, in relation to the adjusted Income of the Owner removing inflexible Costs. The largesse of the Property tax payment impacts as well, reducing Consumer Demand further; as Owners think to provide budget cushion, reasonably estimated to average almost 14% of the total cost of Property tax payment. The total percentage of the adjusted Income must be changed because of the above factor.

Economic studies vary in determination of the total amount of Total Income to be removed from adjusted Income as inflexible Costs. Different Income classes use different percentage amounts of Total Income as inflexible Costs. Increased Income indicates a reduction of the total percent of Total Income devoted to inflexible Costs. Age of Income-Earner also reveals a reduction of Total Income devoted to inflexible Costs, due to removal of Mortgages and high rates of Consumer debt. Business-oriented Economic studies place the percentage of Total Income devoted to inflexible Costs lower than due Consumer-oriented studies. Almost all studies would agree inflexible Costs exceed fifty percent of Total Income for Consumers. The Author finds studies either too low or too high, estimating inflexible Costs to average about 61% of Total Income generally for all Consumers as a Class.

Property Tax impact on Consumer Demand can therefore be placed in an equation:

$$X = (39\% TI)/[x + (.14x)], \text{ where } TI = \text{Total Income}$$
$$x = \text{property tax assessment}$$
$$(.14x) = \text{budget cushion.}$$

Much conflict exists among Economists as to the real largesse of current Property tax assessments for Consumers Today. This Author takes the view the assessments equal almost Six percent of the Total Income of all Consumers. This is considerably higher than the estimate of most Economists. Six percent rate of Property tax would equate to greater loss than Fifteen percent of Disposable Income, which translates into almost direct reduction of Consumer Demand. Such a reduction is unacceptable, especially in Recessionary economic conditions. A Property tax assessment to Three percent of Total Income would halve the impact on Consumer Demand, and could be conducted with a general revision of Tax codes.

The impact of Property tax assessment does not end here, but must also be viewed in terms of Third Generation purchase decisions. A Six percent rate of Total Income brings on almost a Eleven percent Product price increase, after travel of the Property tax through the Second Generation. Thus reduction of Consumer Demand, due to Product Price increase, can be estimated as decrease by another 1.37 percent by arrival at the Third Generation. A Layperson should not become excessively excited by this information, though Economists need be concerned; as will be outlined in the following paragraph.

Consumer Demand is bolstered by outside factors, mainly funded by Credit instruments. A new Generation of Households must be outfitted every Twenty-two years, with each Generation outfitted making up about 17% of total Consumer Demand. The funding by Credit instruments means almost a 3.74 percent increase in Consumer Demand per year, even after payment of Interest charges. The Eleven percent Profits increase in the Second Generation of purchase decisions remains a direct replacement of Consumer Demand, so Consumer Demand is replaced after a Six percent Property tax assessment by almost 14.74 percent. The loss of Consumer Demand because of the high Property assessment still means a gain of almost One percent of Consumer Demand [(.17CD—(14.74Iti +.0137Isg)]. This Equation does not include the loss of Consumer Demand for Finance charges. A halved Property tax assessment would actually equate to an actual real increase in Consumer Demand, as Second Generation costs of the Property tax would lessen to a greater extent than cost of Finance.

This may not seem a great loss to the Layperson, but Economists understand the process of aggregating effect in economic performance;

economic reductions utilizing almost the same formulation as used in Compound Interest. A One percent reduction in Consumer Demand over Ten years will not be a loss of Ten percent of Consumer Demand after the period, but a loss of almost 14%. Optimal economic performance cannot allow on-going recoverable loss of Consumer Demand without long-term loss of economic performance. Excessive Property tax assessments have been with Us for over Thirty years, and may be the resultant cause for the lack of Consumer Demand Today; said Demand not meeting current Production capacities, though this lack may be incited by other immediate consequences.

Many Economists would reject the above analysis, stating House-hold Capital Aggregation is dependent on so many diverse factors; such designations could not be assigned accurately. The Author disagrees, stating Capital Aggregation function derives from yearly percentage increases, with temporary yearly losses directly impacting total formation of assets. Proper economic impact must be assigned to such factors, even if actual impact eventually devolves to only a tenth of the impact over the long-run. The Layperson need remember this is not a normal tax impact on Consumer Demand, but an excessive impact which could be avoided by proper assignment of tax rates.

The analysis for Sales tax rates almost duplicates the above estimates, except for the placement of magnitudes. Excessive Sales tax rates injure Consumer Demand at greater intensity than normal Sales tax impact; and so, could be avoided by minimizing the Second Generation impact of excessive tax rates. The rate of injury is less than excessive Property tax, due to the lack of Consumer scheduling for it, and the greater frequency (Turnover) by which the tax is integrated into Cost schedules within the Economy faster. This Process, though, impels a more rapid Inflation rate, this further amplifying the impact on capital aggregation; though slightly reducing the cost of Debt acquisition, this cost reduction generating a higher degree of Consumption and capital aggregation. This greater ease of Credit under Inflation will not effect the long-term capital aggregation function, though, because of the loss of Consumer Demand coming from reduced return on financial instruments.

Consumer Sales tax rates magnify Profits through the Second Generation of purchase decisions as previously pointed out, so it directly fuels Inflation. This Inflation, because it is ahead of normal Wage scales, also reduces Consumer Demand. The degree Inflation exceeds normal Wage scales thereby also deserves examination. Business interests try to resist Wage increases until the Fourth Generation of purchase decisions, where they gather ancillary profits from Sales tax rates. They are aided in this by the rapid Turnover rate of Sales tax collection, the ability to raise Product pricing with use of heavy advertising to maintain sufficient demand for Product, and the inability of Labor to gather information on Inflation increases. Survival without Wage increase until the Fifth Generation can actually double realizable Profits.

The cost to Labor from this process almost doubles the injury of excessive Sales tax rates. Capital aggregation is sharply curtailed, and is often eliminated in the short-term. Temporary interim costs for Maintenance needs often are raised by as much as Twenty percent, before reimbursement can be obtained from Employer. Repetitive periods can actually reduce total capital aggregation for Labor. The period of the Reagan administration serves as an excellent example of this Process, in that Business interests found it a Boom Era, while the standard of living for Labor actually dropped consistently; until almost Thirty percent of Working Class standard of living had been lost. It must be admitted Inflation held much greater precedence in this loss, than did excessive Sales tax rates; though this Inflation was directly caused by deficit Government spending and the advancing Sales tax rate.

Control of Sales tax rates becomes a necessity, understanding the adverse impact on Labor which excessive rates generate. Is there a Case for elimination of Sales tax completely, with other avenues for revenue generation? It is easy to say yes, but it would not be true. Sale taxes generate an immediate, continuous income for subordinate levels of

Government; short-term Government activity would have to be financed by operating debt without the Sales tax. The Sales tax is applied to actual Consumption, and currently is the only real form of taxation on the Wealthy. This tax on Consumption actually regulates Consumer Demand, insisting on priority being placed on budgetary needs, before discretionary spending is utilized. The revenues are huge, and not easily replaced with economic dispersal to avoid adverse economic impact in the new forms of taxation. The rates still need be limited, to avoid adverse economic impact in Sales tax itself.

A earlier mention of 4.3% maximum Sales tax rate calls for justification, though the Author stated he preferred Three percent rate. Economic studies suggest 4.3% Sales tax rate will raise the greatest revenue, without reduction of Consumer Demand starting to reduce actual receipts. The computation for these Studies is detailed, and takes trained Mathematicians to fully understand; the Author will leave it saying growth of the Economy, as expressed by total Wage levels increments, continue until a Sales tax rate of 4.3% is introduced. This states that normal Consumer Demand will absorb up to a 4.3% Sales tax rate, after which reduced Consumer Demand will reduce it's Wage remuneration for production of the Product. This type of Study is much contested in the Economic profession.

The Author prefers a Three percent Sales tax rate. His rationale for this comes from analysis of factors producing Consumer Demand. This increases faster as the Temporary Savings rate ratio of Workers increase. A tenth of a Percent increase in this rate will increase actual short-term Consumer Demand by Two percent, with a long-term effect of .3% increase in yearly capital aggregation. The expanded Consumer Demand pressures for extended employment of Labor, thus maximizing total Wage remuneration. It does not guarantee prime economic performance, but generates necessary conditions for prime economic performance. Workers must feel they are gaining, before they loosen their expenditure patterns. Short-term Business profits from the expanded Consumer Demand pays for resource replenishment, without short-term finance charges. Collection of Consumer debt under these conditions must be paid by the Consumer, but the continued high rate of Production allows for ease of repayment. Reduction of the Sales tax rate from 4.3% to Three percent would translate into almost .3% increase in total Temporary Savings rate ratios for Labor.

Two of the three major tax impacts on the American Consumer has been discussed. The third major tax impact comes from Personal Income Tax. The Author will defy all Economic thought at this point, and state the tax impact of Personal Income Tax is far too low for an evolved modern Economy. The level of tax exemptions forestall major Tax impact placed upon the very economic entities who should feed the impact, and leave unrestrained their economic decisions because of no impact. Tax revenues are collected from venues which cannot economically support such levels of Collection, all to avoid placement of taxation where it should be placed for peak economic performance. Major economic elements are crippled in economic performance by the revenue collection, while freed elements continue practices of Consumption and Investment which actually raises Resource costs, constrains total Consumption, cuts end-product Consumer Demand losing Business profits, and thereby does not fund hard capital construction. Jobs are lost by the Process, and total economic performance diminishes.

Certain economic considerations need be studied, before entrance in study of the tax impact of Income taxation. The most noteworthy consists of the statement: A static Standard of Living finds base on a flexible, but relatively static, capital aggregation base of the Consumer; or Consumers, when considering the Bell curve of the Population. This provides a real economic implication to economic performance. Consumers cannot, in themselves, provide for continuous economic growth; though they always provide the initial impetus. Their reserve Cash assets, and their ability to obtain Credit, is limited by present assets. Continued Economic growth must be fueled by the Profits of Production. These Profits due this by increased Wage payments, dis-

persals of Dividends to Stockholders, increased payments to Supportive services, and higher tax payments to Government. Failure to
forward these fund transfers will reduce economic performance to a
stability, which may be a increase over the previous static economic
position, but can be equal or less. It is the basic force behind the traditional 'Boom and Bust' cycles. The Bust end of an economic development inevitably begins when Business leadership thinks to cut any of
the above fund transfers; the Economy loses fuel.

Readers may think this is an easily understood concept, which Business leadership would readily adopt to avoid Recessions. This brings
forth a second economic consideration. Economic profits, as opposed
to normal or entrpreneurial profits, are best gained by deviation from
the Business norm. Economic profits differentiate from normal profits,
as they are not the product of the process of Production, but are
extraordinary financial gains obtained by some method. The easiest
means of obtaining Economic Profits comes in deviating from common practice. Economic profits can be much more lucrative than normal profits. The common method during Economic expansions is to
refuse to increase Wage payments, while others are doing so. A second
method is to refuse to pay Dividends in normal schedule, thus vastly
increasing Cash reserves. A third way is tax evasion. A fourth method is
extended delay of payment for Supportive services. Business personnel
traditionally follow normal business practice, until they have eliminated, or paid down, their short-term Operating debt capitalization;
this generally lasts into approximately Ten months of a Boom cycle,
then practices to promote Economic profits begin to appear. Boom
cycles run out of financial fuel, the period of time dependent upon
Consumer Credit capacities. Bust cycles derive from Business leadership greed.

Proper place of Income tax placement can interfere with this Business leadership quest for Economic profits. A number of measures can
be taken, which makes above-noted practices highly disadvantageous.
All call for elimination of the present system of tax exemptions, replac-

ing them with substitutes and impositions which promote continuance of economic performance through utilization of Business profits from Production. The Author will state this is the most controversial of his Proposals, and will meet intense resistance from Economists, Business leaders, and Politicians.

Personal deductions are to be eliminated. The Individual Taxpayer will pay the stipulated rate set up in the Tax schedule for Income. A married Couple will pay the stated rate, unless One does not work. All dependents will allow a Two percent reduction of the Tax rate, to a maximum of Ten percent of the required payment. No Individual will have to pay on more than 2040 hours of Labor per year; this meaning all Overtime is free of taxation. Married Couples filing Joint return pay on 4080 hours of labor if both work, 2040 hours if one Spouse works less than 500 hours per year. There will be no exemptions for Investment or Debt, but a additional Two percent reduction of required payment; if Individual or Joint return can prove payments for either exceeds fifty percent of the required tax payment. Allowed Expenses will not be itemized or allowed, as Tax rates will be adjusted by Tax schedule to account for normal average expenses for Insurance and employment expenses. Proven expenses in excess of $2000 in payment year, which exceeds Ten percent of the required tax payment, will be given a Two percent reduction of tax payment. Individual Taxpayers through the above means will be allowed to freely maximize their Income, without Government punishment for extended effort; while providing fuel for the Economy.

Self-employed and Sole Proprietorships will pay the full rate, but allowed to declare Ten percent of the final tax payment as Overtime pay, without payment. They will be allowed the same Two percentage rate reductions for Dependents. Capital Gains will also be paying the full rate, the same rate as regular Income tax, but will not be allowed the Overtime pay reduction. All legitimate expenses will be allowed equal to Business deductions under the Corporate Income tax. This will have to be specifically itemized. Capital Gains will have to be pay in the same year as derived, at the time of the gain, there being no Carry-forward or backward. They will receive the same Two percent reduction of tax payment, if Investment or Debt payments exceed fifty percent of the tax payment.

The entire range of Corporate accounting practices allowed will be discontinued. There will be no discounting of current Income for either debt or Investment. Recapitalization expense will be split over the life expectancy of the equipment, and will never exceed 100% of the purchase price of the equipment. There will be no 'Maintenance of Facility' credits, only deduction of actual Maintenance expenses. There will be no Carry-back of Income to initial capitalization, Income will be attributed as Income in the current payment year; but Debt service will have been allowed in previous years. There will be no Investment credit during period of Capital construction. Normal Debt service will be allowed, though only up to Eight percent of the amount of the Debt, and cannot be internally financed. Internal finance will be considered normal Investment with no Investment credit. Internal Corporate accounting will not be accepted as Debt extension or service by the Tax system; solely considered as normal investment procedure by the Corporate entity.

The following Chapters will consider various specific proposals for change of the tax system in the United States. The current discussion simply describes the potential methods the tax system can be altered to affect the economy beneficially. The present system evokes all the hazards of adverse tax impact, while denying the potential benefits of tax impact. The Economy is a complex matrix of Prices and Supply, and Taxes incur the same degree of impact as does Product pricing. Readers should understand this means Taxes imitate Product prices, they can be too expensive or too cheap. Either can affect Production schedules too violently. This violence is expressed as Inflation or loss of Production. Inflation destroys the rate of return for all Economic participants, inevitably leading to reduced Production at higher cost. Loss of Production leads to Inflation, as Production does not meet Consumer Demand. Proper Tax placement for proper tax impact is a must!

9
The Wish List

Head of the Author's personal desires for Tax reform would be a unitary, Government defined Accounting procedure. Congressional enactments have enjoined the Internal Revenue Service to accept almost any Imaginary as legitimate protocol. Corporate Accounting officers share techniques which exceed ordinary comprehension. They now use sliding scales of Estimated Profitability, where current Profits can be discounted because of expected decreases of Profits in the future; claimed as loss. Such discounts are set in stone, with no demanded payment; if the expected lost Profits do not materialize. Corporation normally take a Thirty percent yearly Depreciation allowance on hard capital elements for Fifteen years.

Resources stocks are taken as a Cost one year, then taken as a loss the year following as storage expense. Corporations deduct full Worker medical insurance and pension payments, though they make Workers bear a share of the Cost of such payments. Many Corporations deduct Property tax assessments, even though these assessments are deferred in a Free Enterprise Zone. Corporations are allowed to deduct Products held in their distribution network as Expense, even though they charge their distributors a finance charge for possession of unsold Product. They are allowed to deduct this finance charge as simple repayment of an outstanding loan. Corporate Accounting procedures are a Joke, but accepted by the Internal Revenue Service.

Elimination of obviously tax-evasive Accounting procedures would double the tax revenues collected from Corporations, even if nothing else was changed in the tax system. The Reader might imagine such Accounting procedures enhance economic procedures. Nothing could be further from the truth. Previous analysis presented the accurate picture that continued economic performance had to be fueled from Profits from Production, through Wage payments, increased Dividends, increased payments to Support Services, and higher tax revenues from Business organizations. The Last is among the most important.

Increased Wage payments are the paramount method by which Consumer Demand is maintained and advanced; Consumer Demand utterly necessary to continue high economic performance. Increased Dividends to Stockholders fuel additional Investment and Consumer Demand. Increased payments for Support Services spurs additional Employment and Consumer Demand. All produce direct increase of Consumer Demand by additions of Income to the potential Consumer. The Three elements, though, do not distribute more than half of the evolved Business profits; Wage increases to Workers rarely raise Income more than twenty percent of previous Wage, Support Service generally hire no more than an additional Three percent of the potential Labor force, and Dividend distributions are limited by Corporate action.

The real distribution practice of Production Profits to fuel the Economy comes from the higher tax revenues from Business organizations. Business Income is not actually taxed, only the Profits made; unlike an ordinary Taxpayer; who get limited deductions for expenses, but whose operational viability is not supported. Business organizations only have to pay on certified Profits, after all expenses have been accounted. A tax on such Organization is not going to leave Someone without Dinner, or Gas to get to work in the Morning. Their expenses have already been underwritten by Public deduction. Business tax is a Communal demand of a share of the Profits of Production. Most Business people proclaim this is oppressive, but there is the need to propel economic performance from such Profits.

The higher tax revenues from Business organizations fund Infrastructure construction of the Government, which incurs large Employment rolls and greater Consumer Demand through Wage payments to the Consumers. Business is not injured by higher tax payments, as their capital aggregation function depends upon their ability to sell what they produce, and their ability to produce in a profitable capital utilization. Their ability to acquire Credit is not affected by the level of tax payments. Subtraction of tax from Profits in no way diminishes their ability to do business, as it is a tax upon Profits and not Income. Their detestation for such taxation comes from personal desire for higher Personal Income, and desire for more rapid business growth than which is attainable with said taxation.

Economists claim this more rapid business growth allows for greater economic performance. The Author disagrees, stating it is imaginary growth; rationale being it is capital construction without establishment of Consumer Demand to fund the economic production. Such type growth soon outstrips it's market, as it is over-production for the Consumer. This effect may or may not appear in individual enterprise, but quickly becomes obvious in the total Economy. The result is loss of Business profitability, under-utilization of capital investment, lack of Return on that investment, and Layoffs, Downsizing, and closed Production lines. This process enclosed entirely in a spectrum of over-use of Resources, an immediate spur to overall Inflation.

Economic argument insisting tax deferment for Business enhances economic performance is flat wrong. Tax deferment for Business actually leads to over-taxing of Personal Incomes, producing direct reduction of Consumer Demand. It leads directly to Government deficits, the real primary Generator of Inflation. It leads to reduced Government Infrastructure construction, which reduces Consumer Demand; as well as impeding actual economic performance due to poor Maintenance. The over-growth of Productive capacity spurs Inflation, serves as propellent for Bust cycles—leading the Pack in Layoffs and Down-sizing, actually curtails Consumer Demand by competition for Resources, and pulls down other more profitable associated Business operations. The Author does not believe in the Supply-Side Economic argument.

He proposes the Counter-argument that realistic taxation of Business Profits holds the only key to elimination of the Boom and Bust cycles of the Economy. The final goal would be reduction of taxation on Personal Income, thereby spurring Consumer Demand and Savings. The method to get to this Position is complicated, as all things human in operation. Heavy taxation of Business Profits may seem the panacea, but it also contains it's own complications. Such taxation would lead to Wage suppression, counter-productive in the promotion of Consumer Demand. It would lower repayment rates on Capital, with smaller Dividends and Interest rates. Business leadership would be less inclined to expand Production, maintain Production schedules, or hire more Labor and engage in Overtime payments. Consumer Product prices would rise as Production shrank with stable Consumer Demand. Economists know Corrections become Over-Corrections far too easily; Transitions must be gradual and moderate, else Boom turns to Bust. Specific provisions will follow in later Chapters of this Work.

The third great need in alteration of the tax system comes in the complete integration of all Income into the tax base. Splitting of Income by type destroys the integrity of the system. Tax deferments are written for each separate type of Income, all of greater magnitude and number to provide a viable tax system. Employment Wage and Salary, extraordinary benefits and profit-sharing from employment, Royalties, Business Profits, Rents, Capital Gains, and Interest should all be taxed as Personal Income. All legitimate expenses would be normally excused, but extraordinary tax deferments disallowed. Legal rationale derived all Participants in the Economy utilize their Income, no matter how attained, to function within the Economy; as such, it is functional operative income. The elimination of tax deferments would provide revenues, while provisioning a necessary reduction in actual tax rates; this closing the current huge gap between nominal and actual tax rates, which makes the current tax system a Joke. This Author is not the only Economist, who believes a real or actual tax rate less than twenty-five percent of the nominal rate, induces distress into the Economy; not to mention the absolute need for deficit spending.

Corporatism, or Globalism as Some would call it, stands as the greatest threat to the Economy today. International Corporations use their ability to shift funds to subvert the normal economic standards set by national governments. They have literally become the most powerful International terrorists existent; their supply of funds forestalling effective prosecution by local governments. Environmental standards, safety of Product standards, quality of Product standards, and Protection of Consumer standards all stand violated by Corporate activity, in almost all government jurisdictions. The Situation does not require a multitude of new regulations, which will be evaded. It requires effective use of Taxation.

The base of taxation must be altered for business practice. Current taxation consists of taxation at point of Production, Distribution, or Sale. It collects taxes when and where the Profits are made. The direction of tax collection must be reversed. The point of Sales where the Income is made, must be the point of collection; the primary jurisdiction of taxation being the area where the Purchaser pays. The Retailer becoming the primary for tax collection, the Producer resizing to the secondary Payee. Almost all Economists express the thought the result would be chaos, but an effective program could be outlined.

The principal element of such a reversal must be a set tax rate on the Retailer, with specific tax placed on the largesse of Wholesale purchase payments made. It would be a high tax, the Author suggesting Thirty percent of all Wholesale purchase payments. Producers and Distributors could deduct the tax payments made by Retailers, Thirty percent off the Wholesale payment for their Goods; but are themselves subject to a Thirty percent tax on their Cost of acquiring Product or Costs of

Production. Many would claim this is a Value-Added tax, but it is a reverse Value-Added Tax. The tax would be large at Retail level, and decrease in size as it returns to level of Production. Tax Collection, while seeming confusing, would be quite simple in operation. Each level of taxation would be charged Thirty percent of their Cost, minus Thirty percent of their Sales, except at the Retail level. This is their tax rate.

Precise Economic studies would have to evaluate such a tax rate, but certain characteristics can be defined. Thirty percent of Sales should always exceed Thirty percent of Costs, but would eliminate Product-dumping and monopoly undercutting of competition. Producers and Distributors would nominally be left without tax, but the concept is not accurate. Producers and Distributors would still have to pay Employee tax and social benefits tax, Property tax, Utility taxes, and Maintenance Cost taxes. They would not be given tax rebate for tax exemption being greater than actual tax rate. Excess Profit-taking through high Profit margins over Cost, would be still taxed at the Retail level. It provides direct suppression of Inflation through curtailment of Sales. The final benefit would entail the change of venue for tax jurisdiction; tax revenue accruing to the region where the Consumer dollars were earned.

The economic impact of such tax alteration sounds the end of Corporatism as currently operating. Production in poorer Economies for Sale in richer Economies would become impossible, unless the poorer Economies' tax agents accepted the shift backward of taxation. Double taxation would necessitate production in the primary tax jurisdiction, without the necessary tax deferment for previously paid taxes. It provides automatic protection for domestic industry without use of tariff; because domestic production is cheaper than is tax-paying foreign production. Inflation would not entail in the Retail Economy, because domestic production would maintain the same Pricing profile; this profile unchanged because of the taxation on Profit-taking at the Retail level.

Debate will ensue because of claim Retail Profit margins will sky-rocket under such a tax system. It should actually reduce those Profit margins, as these Margins more closely tie with Sales; caused by sharper reductions in Sales with Margins advance. The Counter-argument would suggest such a tax system would bankrupt Retailers. The Author estimates only the Consumer will benefit, as Retailers will have to maintain Profit margins equivalent to the market stratagem of a Sale; holding to a Profit margin of less than Twenty percent, rather than the standard Fifty percent. This tighter Profit Margin will not bankrupt Retailers, though it will have long-term effects of reducing Retail rents, Property tax rates, and total Retail Profits. The total impact should reduce the cost of Operating Capital, reduce the cost of Consumer credit, incur only minimal cost increase to the Consumer under adjust-ment (with no long-term effect), lower Business profits from their cur-rent excessive Highs, and raise possibly Forty percent more tax revenues from business activity. The downside would probably be a Twenty percent reduction in Retail Sales employees; this decrease requiring longer hours and higher Wage and Benefits for remaining Sales staff.

The second major effort to curtail International Corporatism would be the invocation of another tax. The Author has never enjoyed the vogue of internal financing for Corporate growth. He has found such growth to be unplanned, in that proper Investment procedures are almost never used on internally-financed Productions. They clearly express this lack of foresight, as internally-financed productions average significantly less Profitability than does externally-financed production, which has external oversight of Lenders. The only truly observable planning used by Corporations for internal financing comes in the form of setting Product price schedules to accumulate funds. This planning is carefully constructed and deeply impacts Product pricing; Consumers probably paying Thirty percent more of their Income for Corporate products, than Production and Distribution Cost analysis including normal Profit margins would dictate they should pay. The

Consumers of these Corporate products can be estimated to lose approximately Eight percent of their Standard of Living, because of this excessive Price scheduling for internal finance. The effect on Consumer capital aggregation is even more rigorous, setting in a time delay in excess of 2.8 years at almost every stage of growth.

The introduction of excessive Price schedules for internal finance is actually introducing economic profits above and beyond normal profits of Production. Economic profits have been examined by many Economist, and most find such Profits to be advantageous. The Author disagrees, stating Economic Profits are nothing other than Price slavery. They derive from monopoly over Product, with compelled purchase from Consumer need. Economists have traditionally claimed such Profits promoted the Economy. They actually only enrich the Product monopolists, and support a specified Class; at a extreme cost to general Consumers. There has never been a shown increase in Investment, except in luxury Goods for the Product monopolists.

Internal Corporate financing shows deviation from the above discussion, but only in nominal directional movement. Management income, while much greater than Labor return, remains relatively fixed in percentage to total Labor income, under normal Production and Distribution Cost analysis. Management becomes wealthy because Product output is increased, while their relative and actual remuneration remains a set relationship with Labor costs. Economic Profits always express a greater payment to Management, while Labor payments do not increase by the same percentage; often with actual Production stable or declining. Management does not share economic profits with Labor, at least not at the same rate under normal Production conditions. This is conducted in a scenario where Consumers pay a higher price for Products, than they would under normal Production conditions.

Devotees of the Corporate system exclaim the expansion of Production facilities is good for the Economy. Hard Statistics suggest a real denial of this assertion. Internally-financed Production shows low

Profitability, low Sales, unfulfilled Profit projections, high rates of Employee layoffs, and rapid elimination of industrial lines. Losses from such Production lines often curtail the Profit gains from more profitable Productions. Marketing efforts show great expense and low return, because the Product is uncompetitive against superior Product from other suppliers. Corporate internally-financed production consumes greater amounts of capital, with less return on the capital, and probably triples the rate of Corporate Downsizing. Stockholders imagine the growth of the Corporation secures their Investment, and will provide greater Dividends. This is not the case. Internally-financing Corporations issue addition stock at the same appreciable rate as their expansion, without the additional stock being distributed to ordinary Stockholders. The ordinary Stockholder bears the risk of expansion, with absorption of all loss by loss of Dividends; all without receipt of Profits through Dividend expansion.

The above condition can be lessened in economic impact, through a percentage tax on undistributed Profits. This tax should be placed on all Profits, which are not used for recapitalization or short-term Operations expense. The tax would pressure for external finance of growth, while the tax rate pressures for dispersal of funds to Stockholders. Corporate Management would reduce Price schedules to increase Sales and reduce Tax payments; so the Consumers benefit. Stockholders would increase both Consumption and Investment schedules elsewhere. Expansion of the tax to include all remunerations to Management in excess of Twenty percent of total Labor costs, would limit the artificial growth rate of Management Income.

The tax rate on these undistributed Profits would create a complexity in themselves. A rate consistent with a Sales tax rate would not alter Corporate practice, and Stockholder and Consumer would not benefit, as charges would be passed on to them. A tax rate consistent with Personal Income tax rates without exemptions would be highly effective, leading to massive alteration of Corporate structure. Management salaries and benefits would begin to drop, Stockholders dividends would increase rapidly, and Corporate Price schedules would reduce to aid the Consumer. The downside would be shift of Capital from financial instruments to Stock, as dividends increased; driving up Interest rates. Losses to economic expansion would be around Ten percent of the current growth rate, due to higher Interest rates and lessened Corporate expansion.

Lesser tax rates on undistributed Profits would lessen the distribution to Stockholders, thereby lessening the drain of financial reserves to Stock acquisition. The impact on Consumers would remain the probable same, if the tax rate remained above Fifteen percent; Corporate management using reduced Prices to gain Sales. Corporate flexibility could also be maintained with a median tax rate, as small cost increases in Production performance would be exploited. The decline in total growth can be expected to continue, as Corporate management seeks to limit risk when it does not benefit themselves. Government infrastructure contracts and incentives to small business will have to be used to maintain growth rates.

Any Economy stands as a complex mechanism, with innumerable parts which must work in harmony with each other; all connected by some medium of operation. A Tax system must both draw revenue for Government services, and affect the economic performance as little as possible. The last criteria insists on the proper placement of tax rates. The Author believes only a general tax system, uniform in scope and easily adaptable, has any possibility of controlling proper tax rates. The history of American tax exemption specialization has been a history of introduction of dis-economies. Tax revenues have decreased in relation to economic volumes of Income, government deficits with their Inflationary burden provide continuous harm, and Consumer standards of living have decreased as percentage rate of growth. The next Chapter will begin the actual process of specifying a general tax system. The Author hopes he can maintain a balanced account of expected benefits and costs.

10

A General Tax System

One must first determine the Government services needed by a modern Economy, before an estimated Tax system can be devised. We need National defense, legal protections, infrastructure, community services like Fire Dept. and Water, Sewage, and Maintenance services.

We add Educational provision for the benefit of the Economy. The above is a simple statement, but estimates of basic funding vary greatly for these services. Evaluation of extremes, both high and low, suggest there is a Mean around Fifteen percent of GDP (Gross Domestic Product). Provision of some form of Community medical services and Society Security adds some Three Percent subtraction from GDP, if rationally designed. Most Economists proclaim We provide these Services for less than Twenty percent of American GDP. The Author believes this to be too lean an estimate, thinking the cost is around Twenty-Six percent of GDP. He also believes this is Ten percent greater than it should be, basically because of Profit-taking allowed by loose Government Contract issuance.

It was outlined earlier in this Work that Government deficits are directly responsible for all Inflation, except for the extension of Consumer Credit. This demands Taxes fund Government expenditures, whether they are excessive or not. It has also been shown excess taxation will adversely affect Consumer Demand. Economists will detail a certain minimum of Income must be maintained for all Citizens, to participate in the Economy; this is a very important point, for lack of participation is as bad for the Economy as to the Individual—with sharp reductions of Consumption. The above information practically necessitates a graduated level of taxation, where lower Incomes pay less tax.

A unified National Sales and Property tax rate system becomes vital under these circumstances, as these types of Tax are regressive; lower Incomes paying much higher payments, both in terms of their Income, and in total amounts of payment. A uniform national tax rate system for these type taxes will place a maxima upon the drain of these taxes on lower Incomes. An excellent tax placement would be a Sales tax rate of Three percent, and a One percent per year Property tax rate. This uniform tax rate system would assure the burden of Government expenditures could not be shifted to lower Incomes. The burden of Government expenditures must be endured by more progressive tax systems.

Consideration of Social Security must next enter the discussion. Elimination of such Benefits would have extreme impact on economic performance, as previously explained. Support of these Benefit expenditures must be organized so lower Incomes are not unduly taxed. The suggested program is to eliminate the separation between Social Security withdrawals and Personal Income tax. The Law would be simple to implement: simply stating the first Seven percent of all paid Income tax would go to the Social Security Fund. This would require elimination of the limitation of Social Security withdrawals currently in force; this able to be excused by increasing costs of benefits and Medicare payments, making such limitations fallacious. Business could also be entailed to provide co-payment to the Social Security Fund, through a Three percent excise tax upon all Wages and Salaries paid. This excise tax would guarantee the Social Security Fund for another Thirty-Five years; raising Production costs a maximum of Six percent, but lowering costs of Employee and Retiree medical insurance. The Social Security program is further secured, and Consumption hardly reduced; because of down-line savings of scale.

The third great change must be in the designation of Personal Income. Any Income which allows for Participation of the Recipient in the Economy must be considered as Personal Income. This eliminates separate classification of Personal Income, Business Income, Rents, Royalties, Capital Gains, Bonuses, Paid-up Life Insurance, etc. It also cancels all special tax concessions granted to any type Income. The next step is to rid the tax system of all tax concessions for the practice of Investment; IRAs etc. replaced by lower actual tax rates. Personal exemptions would also be dumped, with only a stipulated exemption for each Dependent; as discussed in prior Chapters. All will be replaced with lower tax rates.

The fourth change would be all Income would be taxed. The process of exemption of Government payments, and a whole list of other incomes, will be eliminated. All sources of Income are to be listed and taxed, all the way to Food stamps, Housing payments, and Medicaid and Medicare payments. The only exemption allowed would be private Insurance payments and annuities. Inheritance tax would also be considered as Income, though it is allowed to be averaged over Thirty years; though the payment is due within the year of receipt. The total of change from the above provisions are estimated to raise Tax revenues by Forty-One percent, irrelevant of actual tax rate set.

Corporate Income would be distinguished in only one manner from all other types of Income. Income of Individual need to supply maintenance costs for survival in the Economy and Society. Corporations differ from Individuals, in that they have no maintenance costs; outside of normally subtracted Production costs. This is artificial favoritism of Corporations, allowing discrimination towards human Taxpayers. A maintenance tax of Twelve percent will be assessed on Gross Profits of Corporations, without any exemption of any type; to negate the discrimination against human taxpayers. This is assessed immediately after Production and Distribution Costs are determined, and paid on a monthly basis; exactly as Individual maintenance costs are paid.

The second change for Corporate taxation will come in the form of allowances for normal expenses. The major alteration lies in allowance for Management salaries and benefits. Corporations will not be allowed to deduct remuneration to Management greater than Twenty percent of total Production costs of operation. Most Economists would say this stipulation is interference with Business practice, and the Author would agree. This total of Twenty percent would include all, including Stock options; and designed to maintain Consumer Demand for Product, by limiting extraneous costs having nothing to do with Production capacity. Corporate Management does not have the right to enrich itself, at the expense of Consumer and Stockholder.

The proper taxation to control internal finance by Corporations at reduced Profit comes in the simple provision: Stockholder dividends will be considered as simple Wages and deductible, if Dividends are distributed in the Year in which they are earned. Other Economists will immediately state it should be considered as Interest, but Accounting procedures would be simplified by attributing Dividends as Wages. It then becomes a simple matter of units of Stock, and largesse of return per Unit; percentage estimates and re-visuals do not have to be made. The Corporations will be charged for Income, if the Dividends are not dispensed with the Year earned. The rate they will be charged will be the same as for Personal Taxpayers of the same Income level. Interest rate deductions from external financing would be maintained. Corporations would relearn the practice of writing Investment prospectus.

The setting of Income tax rates becomes more complex, though within established limits. A minima can be ascertained by the Social Security provision, so at least Seven percent of all Income would be taxed. A maxima is determined by the need to eliminate Deficit spending at all three levels of American Government. The Author would stipulate he believes Two percent Surplus should be maintained on all Government expenditures; this to soundly fund the Federal Reserve; said system used to bank the excess funds, guaranteeing a growth of financial Capital stock. A distribution system between levels of Government has to be devised, if uniform rates of Sales and Property tax are imposed. The Author here states this is only the starting point for determination of a tax system, to the probable dismay of the Lay Reader.

The distribution of tax revenues among the three levels of Government can be determined by Congressional district, which are designed by basic Population statistics. Payment will be determined by share minus taxes collected by the District in question, to provide equity for all Districts. The distribution between Levels should be Twenty percent for Local Government, because they have to provide Community services; Ten percent for the State Level, as they have to provide infrastructure; and Seventy percent for the Federal level, though they must see all Government expenditures are paid. Local Communities will receive their payments based on percentage of Population. Infrastructure costs at the Local level will be underwritten by a Fund maintained by the Federal Reserve; who will be assigned obligation to provide Oversight of all Local public construction, both for Population equity and viability of loan extension.

The entire intent of the general tax system is to establish a Fund pool of tax revenues. This pool will allow all three levels of Government to fund developments at their level, according to the desires of their Constituency; but limited by the total access of funds allowed. Deficit spending will not be allowed, beyond funding by loan from the Federal Reserve. Debt will become National Debt, and under the sole control of the Federal level. Extension of Government services at Local and State levels will be constrained by Fund limitations, with a unity of purpose in approaching the Federal level for greater funding. Federal level funding will be limited by the need to share with subordinate levels, and resistance by all Americans; able to blame a singular Entity for deficit spending.

Individual Taxpayers will benefit immensely from the rationalization of the tax system. The paperwork associated with Tax-paying will be severely reduced, with standardized rates without exemptions. Property taxes will be rationalized with standardized payments, low enough all will not be disadvantaged from Consumer Consumption. Property tax deferments will be eliminated, and Business will go back to paying their fair share of local taxation. The uniform Sales tax rate will reduce this regressive tax against Consumers almost everywhere, while still providing continuous funding for daily operations.

The Author will now enter into a tirade he has previously ventured into in previous writing (Plans for the Future, Xlibris 2000). He believes Education serves only the Student and his later Employer, not the Parent or Community; where the Student is unlikely to ever work within. Student and Employer should be charged with the cost of Education, cutting the worst drain on local Community revenues. Any numbers of programs can be devised to charge Employer and Student by the Hour worked for the cost of Education. The collection can be charged to the Internal Revenue Service, and distribution with equity can be outlined. Anyone desirous of more study can check the Author's previous Work. He will simply state here that such a program could be conducted much cheaper, and with far less economic dislocation, than is consistent with the present system based on Property tax; where local Communities have extreme loan commitments for School facilities.

The advantages of a general tax system are vast, and discussion could continue at great length; with boredom to All concerned, especially the Author. One of the great characteristics of such establishment lies in creating parameters of Expenditure for Government in this Country. The current system allows for each of the three levels to organize their own rate of expenditure, violating equity for all American citizens; often making them pay great variance of tax, and often doing without necessary services. All Americans could determine what they want, and what it will cost; often completely altering what they really want. Case examples should be given.

Some intercity residents have Ambulance services five block away, while some rural residents have Ambulance services over thirty miles away. The example sounds bad, but it sounds even worse to say some intercity residents receive Ambulance service at greater time, than due the rural residents outlined. The Author lacks precise statistics, but estimates Local government has one Supervisor per Eight employees, with State level having one Supervisor for every Fourteen employees, and Federal level having one Supervisor for every Sixteen employees. The Lay person would say local level supervision is the best, until one examines Private Sector supervision, with one Supervisor per Twenty-eight employees. It is further damning to state Private Sector supervision is probably three times as effective as is Government supervision. Limitations of funding would bring more effective organization, and higher output of accomplishment. Revision of Government organization is intrinsic with limitation of funding. Leaner budgets will not allow for dalliance or false expenditures of personal Employee desire.

Distribution of proper deployment of Government material comes with delegated funding of limited proportion. Government vehicles record a tenth of the milage of a Private Sector salesperson, and a quarter the milage of a Private Sector supervisor. Many Government offices have a vehicle per Employee, while Employees spend Ninety percent of their time in the office. Police Patrol vehicles average a quarter of the milage when traded, as does Taxis in the same area; with less ill-treatment. Ninety percent of the Ambulances in this Country spend Ninety percent of their time sitting in garages. They are traded relatively frequently for new vehicles. Sixty percent of all Emergency Room personnel simply fill out paperwork at any given hour of time, work shift after work shift. Government overstaffing costs at least Forty percent of Government expenditure. This would cease with budget constraint.

11
Methodology

Here will start the anger of Reader, because all hate the thought of actual tax payment. All Income must be taxed, as stated before, in order to achieve impact. This taxation should be conducted with the least need of paperwork, collection effort, and least affect on Consumer Demand. The Author has considered many types of tax collection, including an actual Bank Transfer Tax previously. His studies lead him to the belief that the banking system serves as the best actual collection agent. Such a tax collection system would resemble a permanent garnishment system.

The actual method would divide the tax rates by 365 days, or 366 days with Leap Year. Accounts income would be accounted as Present Day minus Previous Day amounts, times the tax rate. The tax rate to be applied will depend upon the amount of daily increase. Minus daily increases will be untaxed, nor will they be rebated of tax. Tax collections plus records will be electronically transferred to the Internal Revenue Service, along with a record of the transactions. The Bank will record the yearly record of taxes collected, and provide a tax rebate if total yearly Income does not equal the tax withdrawn at the yearly governing rate; the Bank filing the total rebate with the IRS, along with finance charges for the yearly services. Additional withdrawals will also be conducted at Year's end to pay the proper tax rate; if deposits indicate need for additional revenue. This system may seem quite complex, but is Child's Play, considering the current level computer technology.

A certain number of conditions must be written into law, for such a system to operate effectively. The first stipulation is a Federal law stating Checks can only be cashed at Banks, where the appropriate tax rate will always be applied (estimated at fourteen times the daily rate); it is up to the Check owner to file for any tax rebate under circumstances where he has no Account with the Bank. Retailers could still accept personal Checks, but they have to be turned into a Bank to cash them. A second rule of law must be Employees cannot be paid in Cash for Wage amounts over Twenty dollars a month. The third legal stipulation will state the IRS will only return one Tax rebate per Taxpayer per year, not including tax rebates to Banks. The Banks will be required to notify Account holders the amount of total Tax collected from the Account every year, plus the returned tax rebate or additional withdrawal issued by the Bank to the Account. Multiple Accounts will all be handled in the same manner. The Taxpayer will be left with the responsibility of filing a Tax Return, if tax rebates should be larger; almost all personal Taxpayers will not bother, as the actual Tax variance will only consist of addition of dependents with husband and wife normally not eligible.

Business enterprise will normally file on a regular basis, and will be allowed a proportionate monthly rebate; when filing a running summary monthly Tax return electronically. The only tax rebates allowed will cover actual business costs which are legitimately deductible. The tax rate for Business will be Twelve percent, plus One percent for each $100,000 deposited in the Account per year; until a maximum of $2 million is reached, when the rate will stabilize at 32 percent of Account income. Multiple accounts will be all be handled in the same way, though Business enterprise must file a yearly Tax Return to assure multiple Accounts did not forestall application of maximum tax rates.

A real value for this mode of tax collection lies in the Government Treasuries being funded in advance. Treasuries are paid the maximum tax rate applicable at all times, with the Taxpayers being responsible for insurance of tax rebates obtainable. The Economic consequences of this Policy should be explored. It will cost Business concerns about a 3-4 percent increase in Operating capital finance per month, due to the delay of monthly rebate of excess charges because of legitimate Production costs. Most Economists would claim this is suppressive of economic performance. The Author disagrees, stating it has previously been outlined economic performance is dependent upon funding coming from profits from Production. The above becomes a automatic transfer mechanism to supplant personal Income taxes. A real estimate suggests this short-term tax advance with rebate, would continuously service the Federal National Debt until it could be paid off by taxes. The increase in Production cost to Business would be less than One percent, and would not readily be passed on to Consumers; due to competition and simple repayment of rebates as taxation.

Actual Personal tax would be set at 7, 10, 15, 20, 25, and 32 percent per year. The lowest rate would be reserved to Those earning less than $10,000 per year. The Ten percent rate would go to Those earning $10,000-20,000 per year. The rest would advance by $10,000 additions to Income. Business enterprise would be allowed a more refined scale, in order to allow for normal Business costs. The criteria for the Business scale of taxation will be the employment of two Employees (Owner being One), or more than thirty percent of Income per year going to deductible productive expense. Business expenses have to be detailed, not estimated as is current practice, to earn tax rebate.

All other forms of Income will be ascribed as Personal Income, as it allows participation in the Economy. All such Income will be subject to tax, as it is earned. Investments will not earn exemption or tax credit. The added income derived will be used to eliminate deductibles from Medicare payments. Economists would suggest this would restrict Savings and Investment. The Author here states the elimination will have little impact upon capital aggregation of Individual Households, and Investments credits given to established, wealthy Households are a waste; their investment schedules set by limitation of ability to Consume. The assumption of established, wealthy Households of some thirty percent of the tax burden will raise the Consumption pattern of the lowest half of Income Households by an estimated Eight percent; this increase of Consumption allowing for competitive capital aggregation with established wealthy Households.

The Reader should understand a modern technological Economy has developed the financial institutions and instruments necessary to accumulate Capital, without direct Fund-raising efforts of the Entrepreneur. No singular wealthy Household can fund advanced Production capacity by it's own resources. All turn to financial institutions or internal financing by Corporations. Internal finance by Corporations have been shown to be less profitable because of inadequate design of Production, Distribution, and Marketing. It also deprives necessary return and funding avenues to financial institutions and instruments; and whose Managers wrongly charge Depositors of funds for the profitability of the financial institutions and instruments. This is a hidden form of Private Sector taxation, which should be addressed by legislation.

The final discussion should be over the implementation of a Three percent tariff on all Imports brought into this Country. The first element to be considered lay in it would be a huge source of tax revenue. The Author believes it would present an excellent repayment system for the Government debt held by this Nation, not only at the Federal level, but also at State and Local levels. Proper legislation could direct funds received from such tariff to elimination of first Federal, then all Government debt. This expedient may be the most economically beneficial of all repayment programs.

The economic impact of such a tariff would be functionally minor, when considering Consumer Demand. A reduction of Sales taxes to a rate of Three percent leaves the total Consumption tax on Imported Products at Six percent; a reasonable rate considering most Sales taxes today sum to amounts larger. One must examine the impact on Production costs, when entering the discussion because of foreign Component production. Evaluation suggests such tariff would only work out as increased Product cost well within normal expansion of Pricing, and End-Product cost of such tariff would be less than the actual rate of taxation in assembled Products. This due to Industry's ability to fix marginal costs within a Price schedule. Foreign Producers for an American market will be unlikely to see any shift in Import schedules in the Short-run, with losses in the Long-run coming only with higher competition from domestic suppliers; who receive a marginal relief in their Profit margin.

The effect on Balance of Trade should be much greater. American Exports should expand, even if Foreign nations respond with reciprocal tariffs of equivalent magnitude. The basic rationale resides in the form that Production for domestic consumption should rise by some factor greater than Four percent, without a appreciable increase in Product pricing. The added Profits from this added Production will help defray the cost of Transportation, Distribution, and Marketing in foreign markets. Domestic Consumers find no worsened Product price schedule, while foreign Consumers realize an improved Price schedule. The imbalance of Trade endured by the United States should lessen by at least Eleven percent from the impact of a Three percent tariff, all other Production costs remaining relatively static; this qualification inserted because a Four percent increase in Domestic consumption would apply pressure on Resource pricing. This increase in Resource Cost schedules should not exceed two percent, again fixed as marginal costs in overall Product price schedules. It must be admitted, though, as being only a 'educated guess' by the Author; Industry possessing a facility of passing Resource Costs directly to the Consumer.

The analysis is anathema to great segments of the academic Economic community, who insist any form of tariff remains a restraint of Trade. The Author contests the accepted formulation that tariffs are automatically a restraint of Trade. He can see several Scenarios where intelligent tariffs could actually increase Trade, the above use being one. He goes on to state he is not an adherent of the Global Economy, as are his Contemporaries; realizing the long-term defeat of production for Foreign Sales. Spread of Technology and Education erase advantages of regional specialization, long-term transport of Product maintains escalating Transport Costs, and the transfer of Raw Materials provide the least Transport Costs. Distribution and Transportation Costs will always eat away the Profitability of Foreign Trade.

Production schedule analysis provides more precise insight into the intrinsic failure of Foreign Trade. Consumer Demand remains the basic Creature of Profits made from Production; the majority of Consumer Demand factors coming from Wages, Salaries, Royalties, and Dividends. A significant replacement of Domestic Production with Foreign Trade, progressively reduces the Profits of Production derived by the major components of Consumer Demand. Domestic Financial Capital is likely dependent upon the Profits of Domestic Production, lacking return from Foreign Production. Foreign Trade cannot be financed by Domestic financial institutions over the long-run. Foreign Trade innately incur Trade Imbalances, unless each Economy produces the same Domestic level of Production for foreign sale.

Some tentative Economic Studies indicate equivalent levels of Domestic Production for foreign Sale can only be achieved through imbalance of distribution of Technology and Education between Trading nations. Equality of the above elements lead only to Price schedule competition by alteration of Profit ratios, these already severely compromised by excessive Transportation Costs. This Competition impacts Consumer Demand, but more importantly; it erodes the evolvement of financial capital from Production; directly crippling domestic financial institutions of both Trading nations. Trade imbalances are the natural result. Economic analysis has proven Trade imbalances do retard Consumer Demand, Investment ratios, and Research and Training programs of Industry and Society. The end-result turns into reduced economic performance by both Trading nations.

The advantage of Trade when there is imbalance of Technology and Education between Trading nations remains Product exchange resulting in a balance of these two components. The Author believes there is not Trade advantage above the exchange of Raw Materials, which can be maintained between two Trading partners; that may be continued for a longer Period than Thirty years, the effective time frame in which to train a new Labor Generation under Capitalization. Long-term commitment of Investment to Foreign Trade stands as a waste of Capital assets, if they cannot be transferred to domestic consumption. Domestic Consumer Demand is generally already served by the current level of Production, and domestic absorption of additional Consumption leads to elimination of Production Profits.

The institution of a Three percent tariff on all Imports would lessen this long-term Investment, and the requisite loss of Production profitability. It would return domestic Consumer Demand to domestic product loyalty, without serious differentiation in Product Price scheduling. The added Profitability of domestic production would raise Consumer Demand, and fully fund financial institutions. It would also defray major Government expense, with increase in Consumer Demand for domestic production; though natural economic forces would reduce tax revenue generation as Trade lessened in quantity. Such a tariff would be a definite Plus.

Conclusion

Current attitude towards Taxation tends to condemn the Practice, and seek reduction of tax rates wherever possible. This ignores the fundamental need to fund Government expenditures. Only two real factors generate Inflation. The first factor derives from the extension of Consumer Credit. It produces a consistent approximately 1.3% Inflation per year, unless greater Profitability is obtained by reduction of Production Costs. This reduced cost of Production cannot be obtained by reduction of Wages, Salaries, and Interest; else there is loss of Consumer Demand to consume the Products produced. The reduced Production Costs must come from more efficient Labor or technology. Both require higher levels of Education and Training. Elimination of extension of Consumer Credit to avoid Inflation is untenable; due to severe losses of Consumer Demand, and overall Standards of Living. Extension of Consumer Credit must be maintained, even if the consistent low level of Inflation must be endured.

The other factor producing Inflation consists of Government deficits. This factor operates much differently than extension of Consumer Credit. First, it is not consistent or low level; operating at a geometric progression evolved from the total level of deficit spending endured. This means there is not one singular impact of Inflation increase, but it provides a impact of Inflation increase every Production cycle following. A Lay Reader can better understand by the statement Government Debt possesses a continuing Inflationary impact, as long as the Debt exists. The Inflationary impact is not less than the Debt financing, or Interest paid on the Debt; and not more than the initial Inflationary impact of Debt acquisition in the first place. Increasing additions to

National Debt will lead to an Inflationary impact closer to the initial Inflationary impact, than to the simple Interest paid on the Deficit; hence the geometric progression. The worst Scenario stands as a continuing Government acquisition of Debt to pay for Government services.

Government deficit spending for any purpose will lead to Inflation of high order; worst cases known as Hyper-Inflation. These have all been brought on solely by Government refusal to tax sufficiently to meet costs of Government services. The Monetarist and Supply-Side argument that Government deficits can be equated to debt loads of individual Consumers or of Private Sector business debt is completely fallacious. The basic reason consists in the fact such debt does not advance Production, which the other two types of Debt assume in the long-run. It is simple refusal to fund Costs, like Consumers failure to pay their bills. It is totally counter-productive, in that it reduces the total Profit of Government suppliers by a minimum of the Interest on the Debt, and by a maximum in excess of that total Profit.

The venue in which this Profit loss is engaged comes in unfunded competition with the Private Sector for Goods and Services in the Economy. All Consumers have to pay the higher Product Prices generated, with the higher Production levels pressuring increases in Resource Price schedules. Debt Service by Government, or Interest paid on the Debt, simply increased the competition for Goods and Services; unless the Debt is repaid through taxation, this reducing such competition by reducing Consumer Demand by the Private Sector. The Reader need understand Government is the largest Consumer in any Economy, and if Government does not pay it's bills, all Participants in the Economy suffer.

The economic argument holds more ramifications than most Readers will realize. The geometric progression of Inflationary impact by Government deficit spending can work to the benefit to the Economy. Government repayment of Debt through taxation will provide a Deflationary impact of geometric proportions; this means Prices will drop faster with Government Debt repayment, at a rate faster than the cost of taxation to the Private Sector. Traditional Economist theory states economic performance, especially during Recessionary periods, can be stimulated by Government deficit spending. The Author directly refutes this Argument; stating continued Government spending must be maintained or increased, but deficit spending must be eliminated from the Equation. A greater Economic stimulus can be derived by Government repayment of Debt by taxation.

The current Government policy to stimulate the Economy is the basic Supply-Side policy of extending tax remissions to Business, while engaging in deficit spending. Consumer Demand remains the key element for superior economic performance. Generation of Consumer Demand stands as the primary desire. Tax remissions to Business retard the process of Product Price schedule reduction to generate Sales. Business will not cut Product prices sufficiently to gain Sales, if promised maintained Profits by tax remission. Increased Government taxation directly on the Consumers will further depress Consumer Demand, by reducing Disposable Income in the worst manner—by lump-sum tax payments which must be budgeted. Current Government policy will actually worsen economic performance, by misplacement of taxation.

Use of Tax policies as outlined in this Work will introduce proper economic incentive to actually spur the current depressed Economy. Persistent use of the Tax policies outlined will lead to continuous acceptable Economic performance. All Economists desire a consistent rate of growth which will absorb unused Labor elements with sufficient profitability for Production, so that hard productive Investment develops naturally. This can only come through efficient and sufficient tax collection to pay for Government services.

0-595-27363-7

www.ingramcontent.com/pod-product-compliance
Lightning Source LLC
Chambersburg PA
CBHW030846180526
45163CB00004B/1459